Introduction

The following is an annotated list of books, technical reports and periodical articles related to the development and operation of pulp and paper mills in northern Alberta. The purpose of this work is to encourage members of the public to learn about these industries and their effects on the environment. I hope that readers of the materials listed in this bibliography will become better informed and will help influence the decisions being made in these industrial developments.

The nearly 350 references are grouped into 16 categories. The categories and the items in each category are listed alphabetically. Each category has some very general as well as some very technical materials. Hence, readers should be able to find something at an introductory level before they attempt to read the more complex materials. As some materials may fit into more than one of the categories, the titles of some categories include references to other categories. Some materials on pesticides and heavy metals (such as mercury) are included because their behaviour in ecosystems is similar to some waste chemicals of pulp and paper mills.

Air Pollution	air quality around pulp mills, and general measurement and abatement techniques
Chemistry	introductory as well as very technical materials
Economics	environmental, community and industrial
Environment	general materials
Environmental Impact Assessments	procedures, examples and suggestions about how to improve the process
Fish Toxicology	studies on effluent effects on fish
Forestry	caring for forests and planting trees
Human Health	worker and resident health aspects of environmental pollution
Legal	legal requirements and procedures
Logging	tree cutting and related regulations
Monitoring	monitoring mills and their effluents
Planning	for the future, including accidents
Pulp and Paper Mills	general aspects of design and operation
Waste Management	techniques and problems
Water Pollution	effluent problems and solutions
Water: Rivers and Lakes	quality and management

Most of the materials listed were published after 1980. At least 90% of the materials are available in each of the following three libraries. All are available in at least one of these libraries.

Alberta Environment Library
14th Floor, Oxbridge Place
9820 106 Street
Edmonton, Alberta
T5K 2J6
[Telephone: (403) 427-5870]

Athabasca University Library
Athabasca University
Athabasca, Alberta
T0G 2R0
[Telephone: (403) 675-6254]

Cameron Library
University of Alberta
Edmonton, Alberta
T6G 2J8
[Telephone: (403) 492-4174]

For legal materials, readers could also consult the library at the:
Environmental Law Centre
201 10350 124 Street
Edmonton, Alberta
T5N 3V9
[Telephone: (403) 482-4891]

Government publications are often available both as paper materials as well as on microfiche (photographs condensed onto film that are read on a special reader). Microfiche materials are indicated by their MICROLOG numbers.

Acknowledgements

This bibliography was compiled from computer searches of the Scitech Database (based on three Alberta Government Libraries: Alberta Environment, Alberta Agriculture and Alberta Research Council) and the holdings of the libraries of Athabasca University and the Environmental Law Centre.

I thank the many people, especially the staffs of the libraries mentioned above and members of Friends of the Athabasca Environmental Association, who contributed considerable time and effort to help make this information available to the public.

Robert Holmberg
Faculty of Science
Athabasca University
Athabasca, Alberta
T0G 2R0

May 11, 1992

Air Pollution (see also Waste Management)

Bell, R.W. and D.J. Ogner. *Ambient Air Quality Survey in the Vicinity of Great Lakes Forest Products Limited, Dryden, Ontario.* Technical Memorandum, Air Quality and Meteorology Section, Air Resources Branch, January 1986. Prepared for Northwestern Region, Ontario Ministry of the Environment.
MICROLOG 87-02538, 2 fiche

Gases from the lagoon included reduced sulphur compounds and hydrocarbons (e.g. para-cymene, chloroform).

Calvert, Seymour and Harold M. Englund, editors. *Handbook of Air Pollution Technology.* New York: John Wiley and Sons, 1984.

A technical manual including affects on plants, control of gases and particulates, and source control for pulp mills.

Davison, D.S. et al. *Airshed Management System for the Alberta Oil Sands. Volume I: A Gaussian Frequency Distribution Model. Volume II: Meteorological Data. Volume III: Verification and Sensitivity Studies.* Edmonton: Alberta Environment, 1981.
Prepared by Intera Environmental Consultants and Western Research and Development Ltd. for Research Management Division of Alberta Environment.
Alberta Oil Sands Environmental Research Program (AOSERP) Reports 119, 120 and 124.

An air quality model that uses three components: a time series file of meteorological data, a program that estimates ground level concentrations, and a frequency analysis program to allow examination of various scenarios.

Douglas, G.W. and A.C. Skorepa. *Monitoring Air Quality with Lichen: A Feasibility Study.* [Edmonton]: Syncrude Canada, 1976.

Some lichens (each a combination of a fungus and an alga) are very sensitive to air pollution. This study set up a permanent set of monitoring plots. During the study, 79 species were found in the Fort McMurray area.

Henderson-Sellers, B. *Pollution of Our Atmosphere.* Bristol: Adam Hilger Ltd., 1984.

A technical introduction to air pollution.

Hilborn, J. and M. Still. *Canadian Perspectives on Air Pollution. A State of the Environment Report.* Ottawa: Environment Canada, 1990. Catalogue No. EN1-11/90-1E.

A layperson's introduction to origins, effects, kinds, approaches to study, importance, and responsibility for air pollution.

Jim Lore and Associates Ltd. *A General Literature Review Concerning Atmospheric Emissions of SO_2 and H_2S on Animal Health.* Calgary: Jim Lore and Associates, 1989.
Prepared for Beal Associates Consulting.

This report was prepared on the effects of these air pollutants on mammalian livestock and wildlife.

Keith, Lawrence H., editor. *Identification and Analysis of Organic Pollutants in Air.* Boston: Butterworth Publishers, 1984.

Includes sampling, analytical techniques, environmental analyses, and emissions from combustion sources.

Racette, D.J. *Dustfall and Snow Sampling in the Vicinity of James River-Marathon Limited, Marathon, 1985-86.* Toronto: Ontario Ministry of Environment, Northwestern Section, Technical Support Section, 1987.
MICROLOG 87-06350, 1 fiche

A short study on wood fibers blown from chip piles into a near-by residential area.

Smith, William H. *Air Pollution and Forests: Interaction Between Air Contaminants and Forest Ecosystems,* 2nd edition. New York: Springer-Verlag, 1990.

Comprehensive treatment of how air pollutants affect forest health.

Stern, Arthur, C., Richard W. Boubel, D. Bruce Turner and Donald L. Fox. *Fundamentals of Air Pollution,* second edition. Toronto: Academic Press, 1984.

An introduction to air pollutants, effects of air pollution, measurement of air pollution, meteorology, regulations and control of air pollutants.

Strauss, W. and S. J. Mainwaring. *Air Pollution.* London: Edward Arnold, 1984.

A short introduction to air pollution.

Toole, Gary, Director. *Trouble in the Forest.* National Film Board of Canada, 1991.

This videotape describes the relationship between air pollution and the decline of forests in eastern North America. From the *Nature of Things* Series with David Suzuki.

Chemistry (see also Waste Management)

Crone, Hugh D. *Chemicals and Society: A Guide to the New Chemical Age.* New York: Cambridge University, 1986.

A compact introduction to chemistry for the layperson.

Hawley, Gessner, G. *The Condensed Chemical Dictionary*, 9th edition. New York: Van Nostrand Reinhold, 1977.

A help for chemical compounds and terms.

Levin, Simon A. and Kenneth D. Kimball, editors. *New Perspectives in Ecotoxicology.* Environmental Management, volume 8, number 5, pages 375-442, September 1984.

A special issue of this periodical on the effects of toxic chemicals on ecosystems.

National Council of the Paper Industry for Air and Stream Improvement. *Procedures for the Analysis of Resin and Fatty Acids in Pulp Mill Effluents.* New York: the Council, August 1986.
Also as the Council's Technical Bulletin 501.

Not seen.

O'Neill, Peter. *Environmental Chemistry.* London: George Allen and Unwin, 1985.

An introduction to the major earth elements and their interactions with other elements and with living things.

Ramamoorthy, S. *Mercury Analysis in Environmental Samples.* Vegreville, Alberta: Alberta Environmental Centre, 1982. AECV82-M2.

An example of a protocall for taking and analyzing samples.

Ramamoorthy, Sita and James W. Moore. *Chemical Agents of Environmental Concern in Alberta Waters: A Bibliography. Part I: Organic Compounds.* Vegreville, Alberta: Alberta Environmental Centre, 1982.
AECV82-B1.

A bibliography of 1300 citations on organic compounds of potential concern.

Ramamoorthy, Sita and James W. Moore. *Chemical Agents of Environmental Concern in Alberta Waters: A Bibliography. Part II: Mercury and Cadmium.* Vegreville, Alberta: Alberta Environmental Centre, 1983.
AECV83-B1.

A bibliography of 1100 citations on these two heavy metals.

Sittig, Marshall. *Handbook of Toxic and Hazardous Chemicals.* Park Ridge, New Jersey: Noyes Publications, 1981.

Gives information on chemical names, formulas, synonyms, exposure limits (for the USA), harmful effects and symptoms, etc. for thousands of compounds.

Wardrop, W. L. and Associates Limited. *Poplar Chemical Process Development and Demonstration Facility.* Edmonton: W.L. Wardrop and Associates, 1982.
Prepared for Alberta Energy and Natural Resources.

Potentials for extraction of various chemicals (rather than pulp) from poplar trees. Perhaps some of the byproducts of pulp mills could be used for manufacture of useful chemicals?

Windholz, Martha, Susan Budavari, Rosemary F. Blumetti and Elizabeth S. Otterbein, editors. *The Merck Index. An Encyclopedia of Chemicals, Drugs, and Biologicals,* 10th edition. Rathway, New Jersey: Merck and Co., 1983.

The chemist's "Bible" for finding out basic information on chemicals.

Economics

Anderson, F.J., N.C. Bonsor et al. *The Economic Future of the Forest Products Industry in Northern Ontario.* Thunder Bay: Royal Commission on the Northern Environment, 1981.
Prepared for the Royal Commission on the Northern Environment by Lakehead University.
MICROLOG 83-0302, 3 fiche

Covers North American locational trends, markets and prices, manufacturing costs, wood supplies, and economic prospects.

Beak Consultants Ltd. *Estimate of Costs for Water Pollution Control Measures in the Pulp and Paper Industry.* Ottawa: Water Pollution Control Directorate, 1977.

Dated but covers some of the things to be considered.

Beck, James A. Jr., Richard G. Anderson, Glen W. Armstrong and Glenn H. Farrow. *Alberta Economic Timber Supply Analysis.* Edmonton: Northern Forestry Centre, Canadian Forestry Service, 1988 (revised).

An economic timber supply model including: delivered wood cost model, geographically-referenced forest inventory and harvest scheduling model.

Bormann, F. Herbert and Stephen R. Kellert, editors. *Ecology, Economics, Ethics: The Broken Circle.* New Haven: Yale University Press, 1991.

Includes chapters on: species diversity and extinction, modern agriculture, environmental values, pollution and waste, and market mechanisms.

Canadian Council on Rural Development. *The Relationship of Canada's Forests to Rural Employment and Community Stability.* Ottawa: Canadian Council on Rural Development, 1978.

An old look at how forestry contributes to rural employment across Canada.

Carroll-Hatch (International) Limited. *Market Assessment for Poplar Products.* Vancouver: Carroll-Hatch (International) Limited, Consulting Engineers, July 1983, 3 volumes.
Prepared for Governments of Canada, Alberta, British Columbia.
MICROLOG 84-0790, 7 fiche

Examined: selected pulp and paper products, wood chips, pulpwood, fiber-board, particle-board, wafer-board, hard-board, veneer and plywood, lumber, energy, chemicals and animal feed for markets in North America, Europe, and Asia.

Coban Institute. *Costs of Harvesting Aspen Stands for Energy Production.* Edmonton: Coban Institute, 1981.
ENFOR Project P-163.
MICROLOG 83-2336, 1 fiche

ENFOR is an acronym for ENergy from the FORest, a program for renewable energy production from biomass. Based on work done in 1977, it was concluded that wood chips would be competitive with natural gas until 1983. The research found that felling and skidding costs were higher for aspen cut by chain saw rather than a mechanical cutter.

Daly, Herman E. *Economics, Ecology, Ethics: Essays Toward a Steady-State Economy.* San Francisco: W.H. Freeman, 1980.

Twenty-two essays.

Daly, Herman E. *Steady State Economics.* Covelo, California: Island Press, 1991.

Dealing with non-growth.

Daly, Herman E. and John B. Cobb Jr. *For the Common Good: Redirecting the Economy Toward Community, the Environment, and a Sustainable Future.* Boston: Beacon Press, 1989.

Rethinking economics and economic policies for the United States.

Decker, Daniel J. and Gary R. Goff, editors. *Valuing Wildlife: Economic and Social Perspectives.* Boulder, Colorado: Westview Press, 1987.

A broad view of wildlife's worth.

Dykeman, Floyd W., editor. *Entrepreneurial and Sustainable Rural Communities.* Sackville, New Brunswick: Department of Geography, Mount Allison University, 1990.

Sixteen papers on the economics of small towns and rural areas including discussions on linking theory and action, community adaptation and innovation, and support systems for development.

Economics Branch, Canadian Forestry Service. *Selected Forestry Statistics.* Ottawa: Canadian Forestry Service, 1986.
Cat. No. Fo29-7/37E.

One hundred tables and many figures broken down by province and region. Statistics on forestry resources and management activities, production, export, employment and prices in Canada as well as some information on world trade.

Ekono Consulting Ltd. *Study of Chemithermomechanical Pulp (CTMP) Production Potential for Alberta.* Edmonton: Canadian Forestry Service, Northern Forestry Center and Department of Forestry, Alberta Forestry, Lands and Wildlife, 1986.

Not seen.

Jacobs, Peter and Barry Sadler. *Sustainable Development and Environmental Assessment: Perspectives on Planning for a Common Future.* Hull, Quebec: Canadian Environmental Assessment Research Council (CEARC), [1990?].

Ideas from round table discussions held in 1987.

Keating, Michael. *Toward a Common Future. A Report on Sustainable Development and its Implications for Canada.* Canada: Environment Canada, 1989.
DSS cat. no. En 21-83/1989E.

A short (47 pages) introduction to the environmental problems facing Canada and some suggested solutions.

Nikiforuk, Andrew and Ed Struzik. *The Great Forest Sell-off.* The Globe and Mail Report on Business Magazine, volume 6, number 5, pages 57-59, 61, 63-65, 67, 68, November 1989.

On overview of forest projects in northern Alberta.

Nystrom, Lee, Kobayashi and Associates. *Training Needs Associated with Major Forest Projects in Alberta.* Vancouver: The company, April 1988.

Not seen.

Pearce, David, Anil Markandya and Edward B. Barbier. *Blueprint for a Green Economy.* London: Earthscan, 1989.

The authors are from the London Environmental Economics Centre and prepared this information for the U.K. Department of the Environment. The book covers sustainable development, including environmental costs in calculating total economic value, discounting the future, and incentives for environmental improvements.

Phillips, W., D. DePape and L. Ewanyk. *A Socioeconomic Evaluation of the Recreational Use of Fish and Wildlife Resources in Alberta, with Particular Reference to the AOSERP Study Area. Volume I: Summary and Conclusions.* Edmonton: Alberta Environment and Environment Canada, 1978.
Alberta Oil Sands Environmental Research Program Report 43, Project TF 6.1.

In 1975-76 at least $608,000 was spent in the Fort McMurray area on consumptive and non-consumptive use of fish and vertebrate wildlife. This estimate excludes non-Albertans, commercial and non-recreational uses of these animals.

Prescott-Allen, Christine and Robert Prescott-Allen. *The First Resource: Wild Species in the North American Economy.* New Haven: Yale University Press, 1986.

Economic values of wildlife, logs, fish, trapping and collecting, medicines, food and industrial products, new domesticated organisms, genetic resources, pollination, pest control and recreation.

Wengert, Eugene M. *Utilization and Marketing Opportunities for Alberta Aspen Solid Wood Products.* Edmonton: Forestry Canada and Alberta Forestry, Lands and Wildlife, 1988.
Catalogue No. FO 42-91/46-1988E.

Potentials for other uses of aspen besides pulp: veneer and plywood, furniture blanks and parts, pallet stock, animal bedding, etc.

Environment (general)

Blaike, Piers and Harold Brookfield. *Land Degradation and Society*. London: Methuen, 1987.

The history and cost of land degradation with examples from around the world.

Canadian Environmental Network. *The Green List: A Guide to Canadian Environmental Organizations and Agencies*. Ottawa: Canadian Environmental Network (Box 1289, Station B, K1P 5R3), 1991.

Names, addresses, telephone numbers, mandates, publications and periodicals.

Dahlberg, Kenneth A., Marvin S. Soroos, Anne Thompson Feraru, James E. Hart and B. Thomas Trout. *Environment and the Global Arena: Actors, Values, Policies, and Futures*. Durhan, N.C.: Duke University Press, 1985.

A series of essays from a world perspective.

Forman, Richard T and Michael Godron. *Landscape Ecology*. New York: John Wiley and Sons, 1986.

Structure, dynamics, heterogeneity and management of landscapes.

Friends of the Athabasca Environmental Association. *The FOTA Files: Pulp Mill Pollution and Politics 1988-1991*. Athabasca, Alberta: FOTA, 1991.

A collection of letters and papers written by members of the association about pulp mill developments on the Athabasca River.

International Union for Conservation of Nature and Natural Resources (IUCN). *World Conservation Strategy: Living Resource Conservation for Sustainable Development*. Gland, Switzerland: IUCN, 1980.
Prepared with the United Nations Environment Programme (UNEP), World Wildlife Fund (WWF), Food and Agricultural Organization of the United Nations (FAO), and the United Nations Educational, Scientific and Cultural Organization (UNESCO).

Gives a set of objectives and priorities for national and international action.

Kormondy, Edward J. *Concepts of Ecology*, 3rd Edition. Englewood Cliffs, New Jersey: Prentice-Hall, 1984.

A short, general introduction to ecology.

Macintosh, Rob, editor. *The Alberta Environmental Directory, Third Edition: An Annotated Guide to Alberta's Environmental Organizations and Agencies*. Drayton Valley, Alberta: Pembina Institute (Box 7558, T0E 0M0), August 1989.

This lists the names, addresses, contact persons, and brief description of over 200 organizations and agencies in Alberta and Yukon that are concerned with environmental matters.

McLaren, Christie. *Heartwood*. Equinox, volume 9, number 53, pages 42-55, September/October 1990.

An environmentalist views the "wholesale sell-off of Canada's Boreal forest".

Miller, G. Tyler Jr. *Environmental Science: Sustaining the Earth*, 3rd edition. Belmont, California: Wadsworth, 1991.

A good introduction to the sciences, economics, and ethics involved with exploitation of resources.

Mitsch, William J. and Sven Erik Jorgensen, editors. *Ecological Engineering: An Introduction to Ecotechnology*. New York: John Wiley and Sons, 1989.

Basic principles and case studies.

Oelschlaeger, Max. *The Idea of Wilderness: From Prehistory to the Age of Ecology*. New Haven: Yale University Press, 1991.

When one looks at exploitation of natural resources, one often fails to look at the importance of wild lands.

Organization for Economic Co-operation and Development. *Environmental Indicators: A Preliminary Set*. Paris: OECD, 1991.

An overview of of environmental indices for Canada, France, Japan, West Germany, Italy, United Kingdom and United States.

Owens, Susan and Peter L. Owens. *Environment, Resources and Conservation.* Cambridge: Cambridge University Press, 1991.

A short overview from a European perspective.

Purdom, P. Walton and Stanley H. Anderson. *Environmental Science: Managing the Environment,* 2nd edition. Toronto: Charles E. Merrill, 1983.

An introductory text.

Simpson-Lewis, Wendy, Ruth McKechnie and V. Neimanis. *Stress on Land in Canada.* Ottawa: Policy and Development Branch, Lands Directorate, Environment Canada, 1983. Catalogue number: En 73-2/6E.

An overview of environmental problems in Canada.

Statistics Canada. *Human Activity and the Environment, 1991.* Ottawa: Statistics Canada, Environment and Wealth Accounts Division, System of National Accounts, 1991. Catalogue number 11-509E Occasional

General facts on population, socio-economic factors and environmental conditions.

Syncrude Canada Ltd. *The Habitat of Syncrude Tar Sands Lease #17: An Initial Evaluation.* Edmonton: Syncrude Canada Ltd., 1973. Environmental research Monograph 1973-1.

An overview of the major habitats, vascular plants and vertebrate animals typical of the boreal forest of Alberta.

Thompson, M.D. *Ecological Habitat Mapping of the AOSERP Study Area.* Calgary: Intera Environmental Consultants Ltd., 1978. Prepared for Alberta Oil Sands Environmental Research Program.

Eighteen maps showing vegetation and surficial geology of the study area around Fort McMurray.

Townsend, Colin R. *The Ecology of Steams and Rivers.* London: Edward Arnold, 1980. Studies in Biology no. 122.

A short introduction to the ecology of running water.

Turk, Jonathan and Amos Turk. *Environmental Science,* 3rd edition. Philadelphia: Saunders College Publishing, 1984.

Another introductory text.

Environmental Impact Assessments (EIAs) (see also Legal)

A.A. Aquatic Research Limited. *An Environmental Review of the Daishowa Rail Spur.* [Edmonton?]: A.A. Aquatic Research Ltd., 1988.
Prepared for the Alberta Railway Corporation.

An EIA for the rail line to the Daishowa mill in the Peace River area.

Alberta Energy Company Limited. *Environmental Impact Assessment. Bleached Chemi-Thermo-Mechanical Pulp Mill [at] Slave Lake, Alberta.* Calgary: Alberta Energy Company Ltd., 1989.
Prepared by Western Research with assistance from: E.V.S. Consultants, Kensington Consulting, Ramsay & Associates Consulting Services Ltd., and Fedirchuk McCullough & Associates Ltd.
Main Report. Supplemental Report.

EIA and supplemental reports for the pulp mill at Slave Lake.

Alberta Environment. *Environmental Impact Assessment Guidelines.* Edmonton: Alberta Environment, Environmental Assessment Division, 1985.

Old guidelines on planning, preparation, review, and decisions on EIAs. Notes on various acts.

Alberta Department of Lands and Forests. *Public Hearing on Proposed Pulp Mill Development in the Grande Prairie Area, October 27th, 1967, Grande Prairie, Alberta: Summary.* [Edmonton]: Department of Lands and Forests, 1968?

A very early EIA.

Alberta Newsprint Company. *Environmental Impact Assessment.* Whitecourt, Alberta: Alberta Newsprint Company, Ltd., 1988.
Volume 1 with Supplemental.
Prepared by Nystrom, Lee, Kobayashi and Associates.

EIA for the Whitecourt paper mill.

Alberta-Pacific Forest Industries Inc. *Environmental Impact Assessment. Bleached Kraft Mill.* Edmonton: Alberta-Pacific Forest Industries Inc., 1989.
Prepared by Beak Consultants.
Main Report. Summary Report. Public Participation Program.

This EIA actually has many parts that were produced separately and after these publications. For example see also:
Jack Phelps (Roadway Planning Branch) *Alberta-Pacific Pulp Mill: Roadway Infrastructure Brief* of October 1989.

Alberta-Pacific Forest Industries Inc., Beak Consultants Ltd and H.A. Simons Ltd. *Mitigative Response to Concerns Regarding Chlorinated Organic Compounds.* Edmonton: Alberta-Pacific Forest Industries Ltd., 1990.

This is a supplement to the EIA concerning substitutes for molecular chlorine gas bleaching.

Alberta-Pacific Environmental Impact Assessment Review Board. *The Proposed Alberta-Pacific Pulp Mill: Report of the EIA Review Board.* [Edmonton]: Alberta Environment, 1990.

This is the initial review of the Alberta-Pacific EIA. The public hearings associated with this review were the most extensive in Alberta's history. Transcripts of the hearings (50 volumes) and written submissions (750) are held in the Alberta Environment, Athabasca University and University of Alberta libraries.

Alberta-Pacific Scientific Review Panel. *A Review of the Modified Wood Pulping and Bleaching Processes Proposed for Alberta-Pacific Forest Industries Inc. Pulp Mill.* Edmonton: Alberta Environment, 1990.

This is a review of the above review of the Al-Pac proposal but it only considers the bleaching process.

Bird, Bud and Pauline, Jack and Beverly Macklin, Lyle and Sharon Roth. *Fair Play.* Privately printed, 1990 but available from: Calgary: Maps and Publications Counter, Energy Resources Conservation Board; Edmonton: Community Affairs Branch, Alberta Environment; Olds: Alberta Agriculture.

A short handbook produced by the residents of Eagle Valley from their experiences dealing with developments in the Caroline Gas Field. Chapters include: Talk to Your Neighbours and Stick Together, Stand Up to the Company, Be Reasonable and Cooperative, Get Involved in the Emergency Response Plan, Keep an Eye on the Company, Obtain Information and Stay Informed, Expect Both Negative and Positive Impacts in Your Community.

Blumenfeld, Mark. *Conducting an Environmental Audit.* New York: Executive Enterprises Publications, 1989.

A handbook for doing an environmental audit of a company. Could be used to help prepare or critique an EIA.

Bowles, Roy T. *Social Impact Assessment in Small Communities.: An Integrative Review of Selected Literature.* Toronto: Butterworths, 1981.

When EIAs are done the human social impacts also have to be considered.

Carley, Michael J. and Eduardo S. Bustelo. *Social Impact Assessment and Monitoring: A Guide to the Literature.* Boulder, Colorado: Westview Press, 1984.
Social Impact Assessment Series, No. 7.

A critical review of 600 publications on SIA.

Champion Forest Products Ltd. *Hinton Modernization and Expansion Project: Environment Impact Assessment.* Hinton: Stanley Associates Engineering Ltd. and Beak Associates Consulting Ltd., 1987.

EIA (in 4 volumes) for expansion of the pulp mill in Hinton. Champion recently changed its name to Weldwood. Former names were St. Regis Pulp Mill, Northwood Pulp and Paper Co., and Northwest Pulp and Power Co.

Chem-Security (Alberta) Ltd. *Environmental Impact Assessment for Proposed Expansion of the Alberta Special Waste Treatment Centre. Volume I: Executive Summary.* Calgary: The company, 1991.

An example of an EIA for a plant that disposes of waste chemicals by incineration, land burial, and deep well injection.

Clark, Michael and John Herrington, editors. *The Role of Environmental Impact Assessment in the Planning Process.* London: Mansell Publishing, 1988.

A European view of the EIA process.

Couch, William J., editor. *Environmental Assessment in Canada: 1988 Summary of Current Practice.* [Ottawa]: Canadian Council of Resource and Environment Ministers, 1989.
Cat. No. En 104-4/1988.

A review of the processes across Canada.

CPL Bibliographies. *Public Involvement in Environmental Decisionmaking: An Annotated Bibliography.* Chicago, Illinois: CPL Bibliographies, 1981.

A commercial listing of publications on how the public can be involved in decisions affecting the environment.

Daishowa Canada Company Ltd. *Environmental Assessment Report. Daishowa Canada Co. Ltd. Peace River Kraft Pulp Mill.* Vancouver: H.A. Simons Ltd. and Pacific Liaicon Ltd., 1987-1988.

An EIA in five volumes: the report itself (December 1987), two addenda on their public Consultation Program Documentation (November and December 1987), a Supplemental Information to the Environmental Assessment Report (April 1988), and An Environmental Review of the Daishowa Rail Spur (June 1988).

Derksen, G and M. Lashmer. *Environmental Review of the Crestbrook Pulp Mill at Skookumchuk, British Columbia.* [Vancouver]: Environmental Protection Service, Environmental Protection Branch, Pacific Region, December 1981.

An example of a review process in British Columbia.

Edwards, Paul. *The Alberta Pacific Pulp Mill Proposal: A Review of the Environmental Assessment of a Bleached Kraft Mill.* Journal of Pesticide Reform, volume 10, number 2, pages 14-17, 1990.

A brief overview of the EIA process on the Al-Pac mill up to May 1990.

Edwards, Paul. *The Al-Pac Review Hearings: A Case Study.* Edmonton: Environmental Law Centre, 1990.

A study of the review process for the Alberta-Pacific pulp mill with recommendations for future hearings on environmental matters.

Esso Resources Canada Limited. *Cold Lake Project: Final Environmental Impact Assessment.* Calgary: ESSO, 1979.
Volume I - Project Description. Volume II - Biophysical Resources Impact Assessment. Volume III - Socio-Economic Assessment. Executive Summary.

The EIA for the heavy oil project at Cold Lake.

E.V.S. Consultants Ltd. *Baseline Environmental Studies of the Lesser Slave River. Volume II [of EIA].* North Vancouver: E.V.S. Consultants Ltd., 1991.
Prepared for the Slave Lake Pulp Corporation.

This is the environmental baseline survey of the river and is a supplemental report for the EIA.

Federal Environmental Assessment Review Office. *Manual on Public Involvement in Environmental Assessment: Planning and Implementing Public Involvement Programs.* Calgary: Praxis, 1988.

Includes: context, rationale, support from decision-makers, staffing and organization, and trends.

Jaakko Poyry. *Complementary Scientific Review of the Proposed Alberta-Pacific Pulp Mill Project Environmental Impact Assessment. Main Report.* Helsinki, Finland: Jaakko Poyry, 1990.
Prepared for Alberta Research Council, ARC Contribution Series 1855.

This is a review of the review, of the review of the Al-Pac proposal. It concentrates on the effects of chlorinated organic compounds and biological oxygen demand of the effluent.

MacLaren, Virginia and Joseph B. Whitney, editors. *New Directions in Environmental Impact Assessment in Canada*. Toronto: Methuen, 1985.

Nine papers from a conference held in 1983.

Millar Western Pulp Ltd. *Environmental Impact Assessment of the Proposed Whitecourt Pulp Mill*. Vancouver: H.A. Simons Ltd., Consulting Engineers, 1986.

EIA for the Whitecourt pulp mill.

Parenteau, Rene. *Public Participation in Environmental Decision-Making*. Ottawa: Federal Environmental Assessment Review Office, 1988.

Recommendations on how the public should be involved in decisions made that affect the environment. Topics include: right to participate, various mechanisms for public consultation, and typical presentations made by the public.

Phaneuf, Yves. *EIS Process and Decision Making*. Hull, Quebec: Canadian Environmental Assessment Research Council, 1990. Cat No. En 107-3/16-1990.

Testing the ELECTRE method of determining environmental consequences on a proposed electrical transmission line.

Study Group on Environmental Assessment Hearing Procedures. *Public Review: Neither Judicial, Nor Political, but an Essential Forum for the Future of the Environment. A Report Concerning the Reform of Public Hearing Procedures for Federal Environmental Assessment Reviews*. Ottawa: Federal Environmental Assessment Review Office, 1988.

This report reviews the federal Environment Assessment and Review Process (EARP) and makes several recommendations on the public hearing procedures, intervenor funding, and changes in legislation.

Syncrude Canada Ltd. *Biophysical Impact Assessment for the New Facilities at the Syncrude Canada Ltd. Mildred Lake Plant*. Edmonton: Syncrude Canada Ltd., 1984.

Another EIA for northern Alberta.

Fish Toxicology (see also Monitoring)

Alberta Environment Centre. *Chemical Residues in Fish Tissues in Alberta. I. Wabamun Lake, Lake Newell, McGregor Lake, Beaver River, Battle River*. Vegreville, Alberta: Alberta Environmental Centre, 1983. AECV83-R1.

Fourty-five pesticides and PCBs were examined in 190 fish.

Alberta Environment Centre. *Chemical Residues in Fish Tissues in Alberta. II. Mercury in the North Saskatchewan River*. Vegreville, Alberta: Alberta Environmental Centre, 1983. AECV83-R2.

Mercury was thought to come from former use of fungicides or fish migration from Saskatchewan. This study was used to determine the amount of fish that could be safely consumed.

Alberta Environment Centre. *Chemical Residues in Fish Tissues in Alberta. III. Pesticides and PCBs in the North Saskatchewan River and the Red Deer River*. Vegreville, Alberta: Alberta Environmental Centre, 1983. AECV83-R4.

Fourty-five compounds were tested for in 500 fish.

Alberta Environment Centre. *Methoxychlor and 2,2-Bis(P-Methoxyphenyl)-1,1-Dichloroethylene Residues in Fish in Alberta*. Vegreville, Alberta: Alberta Environmental Centre, 1984. AECV84-R1.

Although these compounds were not detected in the Athabasca River where methoxychlor was used for killing black fly larvae, they were found in the North Saskatchewan River. Their presence there was hypothesized to come from black fly control efforts in Saskatchewan via fish migration.

Alberta Environment Centre. *Mercury in Fish from Six Rivers in Southern Alberta*. Vegreville, Alberta: Alberta Environmental Centre, 1984. AECV84-R2.

For comparisons between southern and northern rivers.

Alberta Environment Centre. *Partitioning of Polychlorinated Biphenyls in the North Saskatchewan River.* Vegreville, Alberta: Alberta Environment Centre, 1984.
AECV84-R3.

Concentrations of PCBs were analyzed in intestinal fat of fish, muscle tissue of fish, fine sediments and water. PCBs were not considered a significant environmental risk.

Alberta Environment Centre. *Acute and Subacute Toxicity of Different Fractions of Athabasca Bitumen to Fish.* Vegreville: Alberta Environment Centre, 1986.
AECV86-R5.

Fish toxicity to oil sand derivatives.

Alberta Environment Centre. *Toxicity of Polyelectrolyte Flocculants to Rainbow Trout.* Vegreville, Alberta: Alberta Environment Centre, 1987.
AECV87-R3.

Fish toxicity to six flocculants in municipal water or coal-mine wastewater was studied.

Alberta Environment Centre. *Toxicity and Environmental Chemistry of Wastewater from a Kraft Pulp and Paper Mill: Fish Toxicity Studies.* Vegreville, Alberta: Alberta Environmental Centre, 1987.
AECV87-R4.

A study on the effluent discharged into the Wapiti River by the Procter and Gamble Cellulose Ltd. kraft mill of Grande Prairie. The fish contained contaminants from the mill as well as pesticides such as DDT and DDE.

Alberta Environment Centre. *Toxicity of Methoxychlor to Fish.* Vegreville, Alberta: Alberta Environmental Centre, 1988.
AECV88-R5.

Toxicity of this pesticide and its emulsifying agent were studied in rainbow trout and five native species of fish.

Anderson, P.D., P. Spear, S. D'Apollonia, S. Perry, J. De Luca and J. Dick. *The Multiple Toxicity of Vanadium, Nickel, and Phenol to Fish.* Edmonton: Alberta Environment and Environment Canada, 1979.
Alberta Oil Sands Environmental Research Program Report 79, Project AF 3.6.1.

Most toxicity studies look at the effects of a single chemical. This study showed synergistic effects of three toxic substances on rainbow trout.

Andersson, Tommy. *Sublethal Physiological Effects of Pulp and Paper Mill Effluents on Fish: A Literature Review.* Solna, Sweden: National Swedish Environmental Protection Board Report 3366, 1987.
Reproduced by U.S. Department of Commerce, National Technical Information Service, Springfield, VA, 22161.

Abstracts of 76 papers published between 1973 and 1986. The papers relate the effects of pulp effluents on fish respiration, oxygen transport, metabolism, growth, and reproduction.

Giles, M.A., J.F. Klaverkamp and S.G. Lawrence. *The Acute Toxicity of Saline Groundwater and Vanadium to Fish and Aquatic Invertebrates.* Edmonton: Alberta Environment and Environment Canada, 1979.
Alberta Oil Sands Environmental Research Program Report AF 3.2.1.

These studies were done because groundwater was to be pumped into the Athabasca River in connection with the oil sands mining and because the groundwater is saline and has considerable vanadium. The studies were done with rainbow trout, lake whitefish, four crustaceans, a chironomid and a mayfly.

Loch, J.S. and J.C. MacLeod. *Fish Toxicity Survey of Four Prairie Province Pulp Mill Effluents.* Ottawa: Canada Fisheries and Marine Service, 1973.
Technical Report Series CEN/T-73-4.

An old review.

Macdonald, G. and H.R. Hamilton. *Model Calibration and Receiving Water Evaluation for Pulp Mill Developments on the Athabasca River: Dissolved Oxygen.* Calgary: HydroQual Consultants, 1989.
Prepared for Alberta Environment, Standards and Approvals Division.

Not seen.

McLeod, C. *The Effects of Methoxychlor Exposure on Early Life Stages of the Native Fish in the Athabasca River.* Edmonton: Alberta Environment, 1987.

A very short term study, but gives an idea of the problems involved in fish bioassays. Some procedures on how to conduct fish toxicity studies.

Monenco Consultants Ltd. *Fish Tissue and Sediment Studies in the Vicinity of the Peace River Pulp Mill Company Mill at Peace River, Alberta. April, 1990.* Calgary: Monenco Consultants Ltd., 1990.
Prepared for Daishowa Canada Co. Ltd.

An example of a short term study of some organic compounds found in pike and sediments.

Monenco Consultants Ltd. *Chlorinated Organics, Water Quality and Fisheries Survey in The Peace, Smokey and Slave Rivers, Alberta and Northwest Territories. Volumes I and II.* Calgary: Monenco Consultants Ltd., 1991.
Prepared for Daishowa Canada Co. Ltd.

An example of a larger study of chlorinated organics found in fish and sediments.

Moore, J.W., S. Ramamoorthy and A. Sharma. *Mercury Residues in Fish from Twenty-Four Lakes and Rivers in Alberta.* Vegreville, Alberta: Alberta Environmental Centre, 1986. AECV86-R4.

Sampling sites included the Athabasca, Beaver, Peace and Saskatchewan River systems. In the Athabasca River, nine species of fish were collected from five locations. Mercury concentrations averaged from 45 to 321 micrograms per kilogram [ug/Kg] (= .045 to .321 milligrams per kilogram [mg/Kg] or parts per million [ppm]) of fish.

National Council of the Paper Industry for Air and Stream Improvement. *Effects of Biologically Treated Bleached Kraft Mill Effluent During Early Life Stage and Full Life Cycle Studies with Fish.* New York: the Council, 1985.
Also as the Council's Technical Bulletin 474.

Not seen.

National Council of the Paper Industry for Air and Stream Improvement. *Guidelines to Methods for the Analysis of the Effects of Effluent on the Flavor of Fish.* New York: the Council, January 1987.
Also as the Council's Technical Bulletin 513.

Fish tainting is seen to be a problem for anglers.

Post, George. *Textbook of Fish Health*, revised and expanded addition. Neptune City, New Jersey: T.F.H. Publications, 1987.

An introduction to fish diseases caused by bacteria, fungi, viruses, parasites, malnutrition, toxic substances and organic wastes.

Forestry (see also Logging)

Alberta Forest Service. *Alberta Phase 3 Forest Inventory: Forest Cover Type Specifications.* Edmonton: Alberta Forestry, Lands and Wildlife, 1984, reprinted 1988.
ENR Report No. Dept. 58.

This outlines the procedures and codes used to describe forest stands. Descriptors include: density, height, species, commercialism, origin, slope, disturbances, condition, understorey and treatment of clearings.

Alberta Forest Service. *Alberta Phase 3 Forest Inventory: An Overview.* Edmonton: Alberta, Forestry, Lands and Wildlife, Timber Management Branch, 1985.
ENR Report No. I/86.

An introduction to how timber maps were produced for the Alberta Forest Inventory (Phase 3) and summary results for the ten forest management districts.

Alberta Forest Service. *Volumes and Stem Numbers for Forest Types: Steps to Volume Table Formulation.* Edmonton: Alberta Energy and Natural Resources, 1985.
ENR Report No. Dept. 61a.

Outlines how calculations were made to calculate volumes of usable wood fiber.

Alberta Forest Service. *Alberta Phase 3 Forest Inventory: Single Tree Volume Tables: Methods of Formulation.* Edmonton: Alberta Energy and Natural Resources, 1985.
ENR Report No. Dept. 86a.

Outlines how calculations were made for Gross Total Volume (cubic metres of tree stems per hectare), Gross Merchantable Volume (excluding stump and top volumes) and Defect Volume (volumes not usable, defective or decayed, for saw logs or pulpwood).

Alberta Forest Service. *Alberta Phase 3 Forest Inventory: Single Tree Volume Tables: Volume Sampling Region 8.* Edmonton: Alberta Energy and Natural Resources, 1985.
ENR Report No. Dept. 86j.

Sample of several technical bulletins for specific forest regions, in this case the Northeast.

Alberta Forest Service. *Alberta Phase 3 Forest Inventory: Volumes and Stem Numbers for Forest Types: Northern Alberta, Volume Sampling Regions 7, 8 and 10.* Edmonton: Alberta Energy and Natural Resources, 1985.
ENR Report No. Dept. 61d.

Sample of several technical reports on wood volumes (cubic metres per hectare) and numbers of tree stems per hectare for different forest types in northern Alberta.

Alberta Forest Service. *Timber Quota Policy.* Edmonton: Alberta Energy and Natural Resources, 1985.
ENR Report No. I/51.
MICROLOG 85-2002, 1 fiche

Short explanation of the quota policy, that is the percentage share of the annual allowable cut of a management unit.

Alberta Forest Service. *Alberta Phase 3 Forest Inventory: Ground Truthing Procedures.* Edmonton: Forestry, Lands and Wildlife, 1989.
ENR Report No. Dept. 53.

Ground and aerial checks on the accuracy of how air photographs were interpreted.

Amyot, Jean-Pierre. *Forest Management in Canada.* Ottawa: Science and Technology Division, Research Branch, Library of Canada, 1988.
Cat. No. YM32-1-87-1-1987-1E.

A ten page overview of the importance of forests and federal government activity in forestry. A good speech with much data.

Association of Canadian Universities for Northern Studies. *International Symposium on the Dynamics of Boreal Forest Ecosystems: Future Research and Management Requirements: Summary Account.* Ottawa: ACUNS-AUCEN, 1982.

Summary of a conference held at Lakehead University in Thunderbay, Ontario. Good for names and addresses of experts on the boreal forest.

Blair, Harry W. and Porus D. Olpadwala. *Forestry in Development Planning: Lessons from the Rural Experience.* Boulder, Colorado: Westview Press, 1988.

A world view of forestry and development.

Bonnor, G.M. *Inventory of Forest Biomass in Canada.* Ottawa: Canadian Forestry Service, ENFOR, 1985.
Catalogue number: Fo42-80/1985

Biomass estimates of trees in various parts of Canada.

Buongiorno, Joseph and J. Keith Gilless. *Forest Management and Economics: A Primer in Quantitative Methods.* New York: MacMillan Publishing, 1987.

A group of mathematical models and computer simulations for managing forestry operations. This is one book in a series on Biological Resource Management.

Canadian Council of Forest Ministers. *A National Forest Sector Strategy for Canada.* Ottawa: Canadian Council of Forest Ministers, 1987. Developed at the Canadian Forestry Forum on a National Forest Sector Strategy at Saint John, New Brunswick.

Set of recommendations.

Canadian Forestry Service, Maritimes. *Can Pulpmill Wood Waste be Used for Land Reclamation?* Canadian Forestry Service, Technical Note No. 170, 1987.
MICROLOG 87-04443, 1 fiche

Use of wood wastes (from clarifier sludge and grit) for adding organic material back to the soil.

College of Forestry, Oregon State University. *Oregon's Forestry Outlook: An Uncertain Future.* Forest Research Laboratory, College of Forestry, Oregon State University, (Corvallis, Oregon, 97331-5703), 1989.
The 1989 Starker Lectures.

Four articles on: forests of central Europe, timber exports, economics and future timber supplies.

Corns, I.G.W. and R.M. Annas. *Field Guide to Forest Ecosystems of West-Central Alberta*. Edmonton: Northern Forestry Centre, Canadian Forestry Service, 1986.

Classification of forest types and information on vegetation.

Cote, Wilfred A. *Alberta Aspen: Tomorrow's Resource Today*. Edmonton: Alberta Research Council, [1988].

A promotional brochure about the properties of aspen wood fibers. Excellent electron micrographs.

Drushka, Ken. *Stumped: The Forest Industry in Transition*. Vancouver: Douglas and McIntyre, 1985.

An outline of the problems in the forest industries in Canada.

Energy, Mines and Resources Canada. *Remote Sensing for Forestry*. Ottawa: Energy, Mines and Resources Canada, 1986. Catalogue number: M77-35/1986 E.

A pamphlet on satellite imagery of forests.

Environment Council of Alberta. *The Environmental Effects of Forestry Operations in Alberta. Report and Recommendations*. Edmonton: Environment Council of Alberta, 1979. ECA79-13/RR.

The Council put forward 140 recommendations, most of which are now implemented or being implemented. However there are some still outstanding concerns such as public participation in Forestry Management Agreements (Recommendation 38), closed system pulp mills (57), and affects of forestry on fish and wildlife (65-71).

Expert (Review) Panel on Forest Management in Alberta. *Forest Management in Alberta*. Edmonton: Forestry, Lands and Wildlife, 1990. Pub. No. I/340.

This panel was chaired by Bruce P. Dancik. It made comments and submitted 133 recommendations on: public involvement, regulatory agencies (Forestry, Lands and Wildlife; Recreation and Parks), forestry planning, forest inventories, environmental impacts, integrated management, and reforestation.

Forestry Canada. *Canada's Forest Inventory 1986*. Ottawa: Forestry Canada, 1986. Catalogue number Fo 41-10/1986E.

Overview of the amounts of harvestable trees.

Gillis, R. Peter and Thomas R. Roach. *Lost Initiatives: Canada's Forest Industries, Forest Policy and Forest Conservation*. New York: Greenwood, 1986.
Contributions in Economics and Economic History, Number 69.

Historical perspectives of forestry in Canada.

Gullion, Gordon W. *Northern Forest Management for Wildlife*. Edmonton: Faculty of Agriculture and Forestry, University of Alberta, 1986.
Forest Industry Lecture Series No. 17.

A booklet on how aspen should be managed for improving populations of wildlife.

Hammond, Herb. *Seeing the Forest Among the Trees: The Case for Wholistic Forest Use*. Vancouver, B.C.: Polestar Book Publishers, 1991.

Covers the interconnectiveness of forests, use of forests, impacts of our use, politics of forests, and wholistic forest use.

Kabzems, A., A.L. Kosowan and W.C. Harris. *Mixedwood Section in an Ecological Perspective, Saskatchewan*, 2nd edition. Saskatchewan Parks and Renewable Resources, Forestry Division and Government of Canada, Canadian Forestry Service, 1986.
Technical Bulletin No. 8, Forest Resource Development Agreement.

An introduction to the mixed wood forest of the southern boreal forest of Saskatchewan.

Kimmins, J.P. *Forest Ecology*. New York: Macmillan Publishing, 1987.

Textbook on forest ecology.

Knize, Perri. *The Mismanagement of the National Forests*. The Atlantic Monthly, volume 268, number 4, pages 98-100, 103, 104, 107, 108, 111, 112, October 1991.

A criticism of the U.S. Forest Service and how it seems to be more interested in timber sales than long term forest protection. Some interesting points on manipulations of figures about economics and jobs.

Luken, James O. *Directing Ecological Succession.* London: Chapman and Hill, 1990.

Introduction to applied ecological topics such as reforestation.

MacIver, D.C., R.B. Street, and A.N. Auclair, editors. *Climate Applications in Forest Renewal and Forest Production: Proceedings of Forest Climate '86, November 17-20, 1986, Geneva Park, Orillia, Ontario.* Ottawa, Ontario: Canadian Forestry Service, 1989

About 50 papers on climate and forest renewal, productivity and management.

Maini, J.S. and J.H. Cayford, editors. *Growth and Utilization of Poplars in Canada.* Ottawa: Forestry and Rural Development, Forestry Branch, 1968.
Publication No. 1205

An old review of when poplar trees were considered as "weeds".

Malik, N. and W.H. Vanden Born. *Use of Herbicides in Forest Management.* Northern Forestry Centre, Canadian Forestry Service, revised 1987.
Information Report NOR-X-282.

A review of the use of and research on herbicides in Canada.

Maser, Chris. *The Redesigned Forest.* Toronto: Stoddart, 1990

This book is about old growth forests, forest conservation, sustainable forestry, and forest policy of the Pacific Northwest.

Morton, Robert T. and Stephen J. Titus. *Remote Sensing for Forest Resources: An Evaluation of Medium-small Scale Natural Color and Color Infrared Photography and Medium Scale Black and White Infrared for the Identification of Selected Forest Resource Features.* Edmonton: Alberta Remote Sensing Center, 1984.
Report 83-1.

The sub-title says it all.

National Council of the Paper Industry for Air and Stream Improvement. *Procedures for Assessing the Effectiveness of Best Management Practices in Protecting Water and Stream Quality Associated with Managed Forests.* New York: the Council, January 1988.
Also as the Council's Technical Bulletin 538.

Not seen.

Omnifacts Research. *Survey of Professional Foresters in Canada. Final Report to Forestry Canada.* Dartmouth, Nova Scotia: Omnifacts Research Limited, 1991.

A survey conducted in September 1990 to determine the views of 2,362 foresters across Canada. Less than three in ten foresters ranked the current condition of forests in their province as excellent or good. Other topics included: forest problems, current and changing management practices, wood supply, harvesting, preservation, clearcutting, pesticides, performance of industry as well as provincial and federal governments, development agreements, and the role of the public.

Peace River Regional Planning Commission. *The Forest Industry in the Peace River Region.* [Grande Prairie]: The Commission, 1982.

Covers B.C. and Alberta.

Peterson, E.B., V.M. Levson and R.D. Kabzems. *Upper Limits of Standing Crop Density for Woody Species in the Prairie Provinces.* Edmonton: Northern Forest Research Centre, Canadian Forestry Service, Environment Canada, 1982.
Information Report NOR-X-243.
MICROLOG 83-2381, 1 fiche

Observations made in 1979 in Alberta, Saskatchewan and Manitoba showed some young stands of shrubs and trees had considerably more above-ground standing crop than was expected from previous studies.

Renewable Resources Sub-Committee of the Public Advisory Committees to the Environment Council of Alberta. *Our Dynamic Forests: The Challenge of Management.* Edmonton: Environment Council of Alberta, 1990. ECA90-PA/CS-S15.

A discussion paper for the Alberta Conservation Strategy. Contains perspectives on administration, management, economics, pulp technologies, multiple users, and sustainability of Alberta's forests.

Retnakaran, A., G.G. Grant, T.J. Ennis, P.G. Fast, B.M. Arif, D. Tyrrell and G.G. Wilson. *Development of Environmentally Acceptable Methods for Controlling Insect Pests of Forests.* Forest Pest Management Institute, Canadian Forestry Service, Department of the Environment, 1982.
Information Report FPM-X-62.
MICROLOG 83-2210, 1 fiche

Reviews insect control by physiological (e.g. hormones and growth regulators, sex pheromones, and genetics) and biological (e.g. bacteria, baculoviruses, fungi, microsporidia, parasites, predators) methods instead of by insecticides (biocides).

Revel, Richard D., T. David Dougherty, and David J. Downing. *Forestry Growth and Revegetation Along Seismic Lines.* Calgary: Univ. of Calgary, 1984.

Gives information of possible use in revegetation of logged areas.

Richards, John F. and Richard P. Tucker, editors. *World Deforestation in the Twentieth Century.* Durham: Duke University, 1988.

Eleven essays that overview the removal of forests in various parts of the world.

Richmond, Hector Allan. *Forever Green: The Story of one of Canada's Foremost Foresters.* Lantzville, British Columbia: Oolichan Books, 1983.

A forester's view of the forest industry in B.C.

Robinson, Gordon. *The Forest and the Trees: A Guide to Excellent Forestry.* Washington, D.C.: Island Press, 1988.

A conservationist's overview of forest management in the United States.

Sanderson, Kim, editor. *Sustainable Use of Canada's Forests: Are We on the Right Track?* Edmonton: Canadian Society of Environmental Biologists, 1991.
Proceedings of a symposium held 5-6 April 1991 at Kananaskis, Alberta.

Abstracts and transcripts of talks given at this conference.

Schneider, Aaron, editor. *Deforestation and "Development" in Canada and the Tropics: The Impact on People and the Environment.* Sydney, Nova Scotia: Centre for International Studies, University College of Cape Breton, 1989.

Contains 120 short articles on three topics: development and deforestation in the tropics, forestry problems in Canada (British Columbia and Nova Scotia), and global impacts of deforestation.

Speight, Martin R. and David Wainhouse. *Ecology and Management of Forest Insects.* Toronto: Clarendon Press, Oxford, 1989.

Despite its seemingly specialized title, this book contains a lot of general information on forest management.

Stoddard, Charles H. and Glenn M. Stoddard. *Essentials of Forestry Practice,* 4th ed. New York: John Wiley, 1987.

A text for U.S. forestry students.

Swift, Jamie. *Cut and Run: The Assault on Canada's Forests.* Toronto: Between the Lines, 1983.

A result of interviews with people who live and work in Canada's forests.

Syncrude Canada Ltd. *Revegetation: Species Selection - An Initial Report.* Edmonton: Syncrude Canada Ltd., 1975.
Environmental Research Monograph 1974-3.

Short description of natural plant communities and revegetated areas near Fort McMurray. Also gives some results of growth chamber studies.

Van Wagner, C.E. *Development and Structure of the Canadian Forest Fire Weather Index System.* Ottawa: Canadian Forestry Service, 1987.
Forestry Technical Report 35.

A short introduction to weather and forest fires.

Walmsley, M., G. Utzig, T. Vold, D. Moon and J. van Barneveld, editors. *Describing Ecosystems in the Field.* Victoria: Ministry of Environment and Ministry of Forestry, 1980.
Land Management Report #7, RAB Technical Paper 2.

An excellent field guide useful for describing forests.

Waring, Richard H. and William H. Schlesinger. *Forest Ecosystems: Concepts and Management.*

Toronto: Academic Press, 1985.

A specialized textbook; considerable physiology of trees.

Westworth, D.A. and Associates. *Significant Natural Features of the Eastern Boreal Forest Region of Alberta.* Edmonton: Alberta Forestry, Lands and Wildlife Technical Report, 1990.

The Westworth report includes The Slave Lake, Athabasca and Lac La Biche Forest Regions (i.e. the FMA for Al-Pac). It lists 614 sites that possess "significant natural features", i.e. fish habitat and aquatic features, vegetation and terrain features, or wildlife habitat.

Wheaton, E.E. and T. Singh. *Exploring the Implications of Climatic Change for the Boreal Forest and Forestry Economics of Western Canada. Development and Demonstration Facility.* Downsview, Ontario: Climate Change Digest, Atmospheric Environment Service, Environment Canada, 1988.
CCD document 89-02.
Environment Canada document En57-27/1989-02.
Saskatchewan Research Council document E-906-61-A-88.

An 18 page summary of "An Exploration and Assessment of the Implications of Climatic Change for the Boreal Forest and Forestry Economics of the Prairie Provinces and Northwest Territories: Phase One" by E.E. Wheaton, T. Singh, R. Dempster, K.O. Higginbotham, J.P. Thorpe, G.C. Van Kooten, and J.S. Taylor. One major prediction is that, because of global warming, the southern edge of the boreal forest may shift northwards between 250 and 900 km.

Human Health (see also Chemistry and Planning)

Bertazzi, P.A., C. Zocchetti, A.C. Pesatori, S. Guercilena, M. Sanarico and L. Radice. *Ten-Year Mortality Study of the Population Involved in the Seveso Incident in 1976.* American Journal of Epidemiology, volume 129, number 6, pages 1187-1200, 1989.

Exposure to dioxins and other chemicals from the accident did increase the number of human cases of cancer.

Dykes, Robert H., Eric Jeffries, Marc D. Sherkin, and Donald F. Stark. *Coming Up for Air: A Survey of the Literature on Air Pollution and Its Effects on Human Health and A Discussion of Ambient Air Readings in Prince George, British Columbia and Their Relationship to Hospital Admissions.* Prince George, B.C.: [Robert H. Dykes?], 1987.

Local medical concerns to the pulp mills of Prince George.

Environ Corp. *Dioxin: Critical Review of Its Distribution, Mechanism of Action, Impacts on Human Health, and the Setting of Acceptable Exposure Limits.* New York: National Council of the Paper Industry for Air and Stream Improvement, Special Report 87-07, 1987.

Impacts on human health have to be reconsidered after recent allegations of fraud in some key studies. See Van Strum and Merrell below.

Hawks, M.P.G. *Health Effects from Kraft (Sulphate) Pulp Mill Operations.* Edmonton: Environment Conservation Authority, 1976.

Old study of literature.

Lave, Lestor. B. and Arthur C. Upton, editors. *Toxic Chemicals, Health, and the Environment.* Baltimore: Johns Hopkins University Press, 1987.

Ten general papers on environmental and health effects of toxic chemicals.

Merrell, Paul and Carol Van Strum. *Negligible Risk: Premeditated Murder?* Journal of Pesticide Reform, volume 10, number 1, pages 20-22, Spring 1990.

A quick look at risk assessment.

National Technical Information Service. *Pulp and Paper Mill Effluents: Toxicity to Humans. (Jan. 76 - Jan. 87).* Springfield, Virginia: The service, February 1987.

A review.

O'Brien, Mary. *If Not Risk Assessment, Then What?* Journal of Pesticide Reform, volume 10, number 1, pages 2-7, Spring 1990.

Promotes qualitative assessment of risks.

Schwartz, E. *A Proportionate Mortality Ratio Analysis of Pulp and Paper Mill Workers in New Hampshire.* British Journal of Industrial Medicine, volume 45, pages 234-238, 1988.

Analysis of 1,071 deaths of pulp and paper workers showed proportionately more deaths from cancers. Mortality analysis of 452 timber cutters and loggers showed no such increases.

Van Strum, Carol and Paul Merrell. *Dioxin Human Health Damage Studies: Damaged Data?* Journal of Pesticide Reform, volume 10, number 1, pages 8-12, Spring 1990.

Overview of the investigations that indicate fraud occurred in several studies of industrial accidents upon which safe levels of dioxins were based.

Wein, Eleanor E. *Nutrient Intakes and Use of Country Foods by Native Canadians Near Wood Buffalo National Park.* Guelph: doctoral thesis, University of Guelph, 1989.

Shows high use of fish for food by natives. Contamination of fish could lead to adverse health effects.

Zack, Judith A. and Raymond R. Suskind. *The Mortality Experience of Workers Exposed to Tetrachlorodibenzodioxin in a Trichlorophenol Process Accident.* Journal of Occupational Medicine, volume 22, number 1, pages 11-14, January 1980.

Mortality analysis on 121 workers involved in an accident at the Monsanto Company plant in Nitro, West Virginia. The validity of this study has been called into question.

Legal (see also EIAs)

Alberta, Province of. *Clean Air Act. Revised Statutes of Alberta 1980, Chapter C-12 with Amendments in force as of August 1, 1985.* Edmonton: Queen's Printer, 1987.

The act that controlled air pollution in Alberta.

Alberta, Province of. *Clean Water Act. Revised Statutes of Alberta 1980, Chapter C-13 with Amendments in force as of August 1, 1985.* Edmonton: Queen's Printer, 1987.

The act that controlled water pollution in Alberta.

Alberta, Province of. *Forests Act.* and *Forest Management Agreements* (section 16 of Forests Act). Edmonton: Queen's Printer, various dates.

The Forest Act controls regulations on the use of the province's forests. The Forest Management Agreements (FMAs) are made between the Province and individual companies. FMAs include definition of the Forest Management Area, withdrawals of land from the agreement, rights over land, cut periods, reforestation, forest protection, charges and dues, and mill construction and operation. For example, Order in Council 575/86 was made with Weldwood of Canada in 1986 and O.C. 778/88 was with Proctor & Gamble Inc. in 1988.

Bankes, N.D. *Crown Timber Rights in Alberta.* The Canadian Institute of Resources Law Working Paper 10. Calgary: Faculty of Law, University of Calgary, 1986.

Legal aspects of selling the forests of Alberta: Forest Management Agreements, Pulpwood Agreements, quotas, and licenses.

Barton, Barry and Barbara Roulston. *A Guide to Appearing Before the Surface Rights Board of Alberta.* The Canadian Institute of Resources Law Working Paper 11. Calgary: Faculty of Law, University of Calgary, 1986.

Information on hearings and compensation.

Duncan, Linda F. *Environmental Enforcement.* Edmonton: Environmental Law Centre, 1984. Proceedings of the National Conference on the Enforcement of Environmental law.

Approaches to enforcement and compliance in Canada.

Duncan, Linda F. *Cradle to Grave. Regulation of Toxic Substances in the Prairie Provinces. A Legal Overview.* Edmonton: Environmental Law Centre, 1985.

Includes: importation, manufacture, storage, transportation, pollution, emergencies.

Duncan, Linda F. *Enforcing Environmental Law: A Guide to Private Prosecution.* Edmonton: Environmental Law Centre, 1990.

A layperson's guide to private prosecution.

Elder, P.S. *Environmental Impact Assessment in Alberta.* Alberta Law Review, volume 23, number 2, pages 286-309, 1985.

A legal critique of the EIA process that points out several areas that could be improved.

Environment Canada. *Canadian Environmental Protection Act: Enforcement and Compliance Policy.* Ottawa: Environment Canada, 1988. En 40-356/1988E.

A layperson's guide to this federal legislation.

Environment Council of Alberta. *Alberta's Clean Water Act. Conclusions and Recommendations of the Review of the Clean Water Act.* Edmonton: Environment Council of Alberta, 1985. ECA86-St/2.

Gives 12 recommendations to improve the implementation and administration of the act.

Flett, Jullian, editor. *Law and Policy Related to the Management of Hazardous Waste in the Province of Alberta.* Edmonton: Environmental Law Centre, 1983.

Proceedings of round table discussions on: siting hazardous waste disposal sites, obtaining compliance, plant closure activities, victim compensation, emergency spill response, avoidance and recycling of hazardous wastes.

Flett, Jillian and Dan Rogers. *The Environmental Legal Action Handbook: A Citizen's Guide to Legal Action.* Edmonton: Student Legal Services, 1980.

The Acts are old but the possible actions are not.

Malvern, R.J., W.M. Paterson and W.J. Platt. *A Reference Guide to Environmental Legislation in Canada (1989 Update).* Ontario Hydro, Environmental Studies and Assessments Department, Report No. 90212, 1990.

A concise listing of provincial and federal acts that deal with environmental issues, including: assessment, air, water, land, noise, wildlife and heritage.

Moen, Andrea B. *Demystifying Forestry Law: An Alberta Analysis.* Edmonton: Alberta Law Centre, 1990.

Discusses ownership, regulation and management including: disposition of timber, Forest Management Agreements, reforestation, enforcement and environmental concerns.

Review Panel for Environmental Law Enforcement. *An Action Plan for Environmental Law Enforcement in Alberta.* Edmonton: Alberta Environment, 1988.

Recommendations on standards setting, air and water quality standards, licensing procedures and requirements, monitoring compliance, non-compliance, prosecution, offenses and penalties, and the Environment Enforcement Unit.

Swanson, Elizabeth and Elaine Hughes. *The Price of Pollution: Environmental Litigation.* Edmonton: Environmental Law Centre, 1990.

Canadian law with respect to pollution, including tort actions, statutory actions and environmental prosecutions.

Tingley, Donna, editor. *Environmental Protection and the Canadian Constitution.* Edmonton: Environmental Law Centre, 1987. Proceedings of the Canadian Symposium on Jurisdiction and Responsibility for the Environment.

Environmental perspectives by various levels of government, industry and the public on the constitutional framework, policies, administration of policies, and future directions.

Tingley, Donna, editor. *Into the Future: Environmental Law and Policy for the 1990's.* Edmonton: Environmental Law Centre, 1990.

Proceedings of a national conference.

Vomberg, Mac. *Bibliography of Legal Materials on Transportation of Hazardous Substances.*

Edmonton: Environmental Law Centre, 1982.

Seven pages of cases, articles and acts. There are many implications for the transport of chemicals to pulp mills.

Zimmerman, Rae. *Governmental Management of Chemical Risk: Regulatory Processes for Environmental Health.* Lewis Publishers, 1990.

American federal law and incentives.

Logging (see also Forestry)

Anderson, Phillip and Robert Anderson. *Erosion Potential Index. A Method for Evaluating Sheet Erosion at Stream Crossings.* Edmonton: Forest Service, Alberta Forestry, Lands and Wildlife, 1987.
ENR Report Number T/137.

How to estimate the potential of soil erosion at stream crossings and how to reduce the damage.

Anderson, Robert A. and David Asquin. *Culvert Sizing for Stream Crossings: A Handbook of Three Common Methods.* Edmonton: Alberta Forestry, Lands and Wildlife, Forestry Services, 1986.

Regulations on sizes and positions of culverts for logging and other roads that need to cross steams.

Coulombe, R. and A.B. Lemay. *Evaluation of Potential Interactions Between Forest Biomass Production and Canadian Wildlife.* Ottawa: Environment Canada, 1983.
ENFOR Project P-170.
Contractor: le Groupe Dryade ltee.
MICROLOG 83-4446, 4 fiche

ENFOR is an acronym for ENergy from the FORest, a program for renewable energy production from biomass. Reviews extending forest cutting rotations, removal of snags and fallen trees, sensitivity of animals to human disturbances, and calls for more research in Canada. Concentrates on vertebrates.

Culp, J.M. and R.W. Davies. *An Assessment of the Effects of Streambank Clear-Cutting on Macroinvertebrate Communities in a Managed Watershed.* Canadian Technical Report of Fisheries and Aquatic Systems No. 1208, 1983.
MICROLOG 84-0471, 2 fiche
Cat. No. Fs 97-6/1208

Studies on on a creek on Vancouver Island. Logging without a buffer zone increased soil erosion and hence sediments in the creek. Increased sediments and reduced detritus decreased numbers of organisms. Lack of a buffer zone also increased winter scouring which also decreased populations. A less than 10 m riparian buffer zone and natural debris dams provided leaf litter and so more food for invertebrates and fish.

Curtin, Theodore W. *Farm Your Forest.* Urbana-Champaign, Illinois: Cooperative Extension Service Circular 1291, College of Agriculture, University of Illinois, 1989.

A pamphlet for managing private wood lots.

Curtis, David S. *Woodlot Owner Organizations in Eastern Canada: Historic Development, Legislation, Structure, Financing and Services.* Fredericton, New Brunswick: Canadian Forestry Services - Maritimes, 1987.
Information Report M-X-162.
MICROLOG 87-03020, 2 fiche

In Nova Scotia, Prince Edward Island, New Brunswick, Quebec and Ontario land owners who sell trees for pulp and lumber have formed various organizations to help market their products and share resources for forest management activities.

Fisher, G.L. *Resource Road Planning Guidelines for the Green Area of Alberta.* Edmonton: Alberta Energy and Natural Resources, Forest Service, 1985.
ENR Technical Report Number T/25.

Recommendations for five kinds of roads used by timber and petroleum industries.

Fisher, G.L., A.G.H. Locke, and B.C. Northey. *Stream Crossing Guidelines: Operational Guidelines for Industry.* Edmonton: Alberta Energy and Natural Resources, Forest Service, 1985.
ENR Technical Report Number T/80.

Recommendations for building, maintaining, and abandoning stream crossings.

Forest Land Use Branch. *The Resource Handbook Operational Guidelines for Industry,* revised.

Edmonton: Alberta Energy and Natural Resources, Forest Service, 1984. ENR Technical Report Number 75.

Recommendations for industries making utility corridors and stream crossings in the forests of Alberta.

Forest Service. *Forest Landscape Management Guidelines for Alberta.* Edmonton: Alberta Forestry, Lands and Wildlife, 1986.

The department's recommendations to reduce the visual impacts of logging.

Forest Service. *Predisturbance Watershed Assessment Manual.* Edmonton: Alberta Forestry, Lands and Wildlife, 1986. ENR Technical Report Number T/100.

The department's recommendations to reduce erosion in watersheds being logged. The recommendations are to be used in the development of Annual Operating Plans (AOPs).

Forest Service. *Alberta Timber Harvest Planning and Operating Ground Rules.* Edmonton: Alberta Forestry, Lands and Wildlife, 1987. ENR Technical Report Number 23.

These are the regulations to be followed by loggers with respect to such things as: Annual Operating Plans, setbacks from water courses, reforestation, wildlife habitat considerations, road construction and abandonment, campsites, and waste disposal.

Moore, G.C. and S.G. Henley. *Final Report of G.D.A. Projects 144.201 and 144.202: Management of Watercourse Buffer Zones.* Fredericton, N.B.: Natural Resources, New Brunswick and Government of Canada, Regional Economic Expansion, 1984. MICROLOG 84-4003, 2 fiche

Experiments and recommendations on management of buffer zones.

Raphael, Ray. *Tree Talk: The People and Politics of Timber.* Covelo, California: Island Press, 1981.

Interviews and ideas on the history, problems and future of logging in the United States.

Sauder, B.J. *Low-Ground-Pressure Tires for Skidders.* Ottawa: Canadian Forestry Service, 1985. Information Report DPC-X-20

A study on these tires which are supposed to lessen soil compaction.

Swanson, Robert H. and Graham Robin Hillman. *Predicted Increased Water Yield After Clear-Cutting Verified in West-Central Alberta.* Edmonton: Northern Forest Research Centre, Canadian Forestry Service NOR-X-198, 1977.

Research done on the effects of clear-cutting.

Monitoring (see also Fish Toxicology)

Alberta Environment. *Dissolved Oxygen Objectives Workshop, Technical Proceedings, 12 December 1989.* Edmonton: Alberta Environmental Protection Services, Environmental Assessment Division, Standards Research and Development Branch, [1990].

Includes: objectives and guidelines, monitoring of rivers and lakes, biochemical oxygen demand, fish protection, physiological responses, and research needs.

Barton, D.R. and R.R. Wallace. *Ecological Studies of the Aquatic Invertebrates of the Alberta Oil Sands Environmental Research Program Study Area of Northeastern Alberta.* Edmonton: Alberta Environment and Environment Canada, 1980. AOSERP Report 88, Project AF 2.0.1.

A baseline study of the aquatic invertebrates of the Athabasca, Muskeg and Steepbank Rivers.

Beak Consultants. *Secondary Fibers Pulping/Deinking Effluent Toxicity Study.* Ottawa: Environment Canada, Environmental Protection Service, Water Pollution Control Directorate, Abatement and Compliance Branch, 1979.

About re-cycled paper.

Beaver, R. and M. Ballantyne. *Breeding Behaviour of the White Pelican in the Athabasca Oil Sands Area.* Edmonton: Alberta Environment and Environment Canada, 1979. Alberta Oil Sands Environmental Research Program Report 82, Project LS 22.2.

White pelicans are fish-eating birds. Their eggs and tissues can be used to monitor toxic substances in water bodies. This report gives some behavioural information on these birds. See also D. Ealey. *The Distribution, Foraging Behaviour, and Allied Activities of the White Pelican in the Athabasca Oil Sands Area.* AOSERP Report 83.

Boerger, Hans. *Distribution and Abundance of Macrobenthos in the Athabasca River near Fort McMurray.* Edmonton: Research Management Division, Alberta Environment, 1983. Report OF-53.

Intended for monitoring water quality with aquatic macroinvertebrates. Chironomids, mayflies, oligochaets, caddisflies and stoneflies comprised 53%, 21%, 18%, 2% and 1% of the 27,229 specimens collected in a 85 km stretch one summer. Densities reached 3,294 individuals per square metre. Densities decreased 31% downstream of the Suncor Tar Sands plant.

Bond, W.A. *Fishery Resources of the Athabasca River Downstream of Fort McMurray: Volume I.* Edmonton: Alberta Environment and Environment Canada, 1980. Alberta Oil Sands Environmental Research Program Report 89, Project AF 4.3.2.

Twenty-seven species of fish were found, 11 of which were common. Diversity reduced to 18 species at the Athabasca Delta. Walleye, Goldeye, Long-Nose Sucker and White Sucker migrate upstream in spring even under ice cover. Lake Whitefish migrate upstream in the fall to spawn. Best introduction to the biology of the fish in the Athabasca River.

Bond, W.A. and K. Machniak. *An Intensive Study of the Fish Fauna of the Steepbank Muskeg River Watershed of Northeastern Alberta.* Edmonton: Alberta Environment and Environment Canada, 1979. Alberta Oil Sands Environmental Research Program Report 76, Project AF 4.5.1.

A similar study to Machniak and Bond, see below. White and Longnose Suckers seem to be part of the Lake Athabasca population, at least 150 km to the north.

Bush, Maureen. *Public Participation in Resource Development After Project Approval.* Hull, Quebec: Canadian Environmental Assessment Research Council, 1990. Cat. No. En 107-3/ 17-1990.

Eight case studies were looked at AFTER the projects were approved and developed.

Byrtus, G. *Athabasca River Monitoring Program - 1981.* Edmonton: Alberta Environment, Pollution Control Division, 1982.

A sample of the monitoring carried out when methoxychlor was being used to kill black fly larvae in the Athabasca River.

Day, K.E., E.D. Ongley, R.P. Scroggins and H.R. Eisenhauer, editors. *Biology in the New Regulatory Framework for Aquatic Protection.* Ottawa: Environment Canada, Environmental Protection, 1989? Proceedings of the Alliston Workshop cosponsored by Environment Canada and the National Water Research Institute, 26-28 April 1988.

Recommendations on the biological criteria (toxicity tests) used to achieve aquatic environmental protection.

Flannagan, John F. *Life Cycles of Some Common Aquatic Insects of the Athabasca River, Alberta.* Edmonton: Alberta Environment and Environment Canada, 1977. Alberta Oil Sands Environmental Research Program Report AF 2.2.1.

Life cycle studies were carried out on 7 species of stoneflies, 7 mayflies and 8 caddisflies at Fort McMurray. These studies were disrupted in July and August 1977, presumably because of black fly control measure done 450 km upstream at Athabasca.

Fransen, M.A.H., R.T. Franson, and A.R. Lucas. *Environmental Standards: a Comparative Study of Canadian Standards, Standard Setting Processes and Enforcement.* Edmonton: Environment Council of Alberta, 1982. ECA83-SP/1.

Outlines how standards, such as effluent limitations, are set. Many of the standards given are out of date.

Hartland-Rowe, R.C.B., R.W. Davies, M.McElhone, and R. Crowther. *The Ecology of Macrobenthic Invertebrate Communities in Hartley Creek, Northeastern Alberta.* Edmonton: Alberta Environment and Environment Canada, 1979. Alberta Oil Sands Environmental Research Program Report WS 1.3.3.

This creek is a tributary of Muskeg River which in turn is a tributary of the Athabasca River. Over 160 species of macroinvertebrates were collected. Chironomids were most abundant but caddisflies had the most biomass. Several distinctive communities were identified. Most insects had one year life cycles. There was a typical diel drift cycle.

Jones, M.L., G.J. Mann and P.J. McCart. *Fall Fisheries Investigations in the Athabasca and Clearwater Rivers Upstream of Fort McMurray. Volume I.* Calgary: Aquatic Environments Ltd., 1978.
Alberta Oil Sands Environmental Research Program Project AF 4.8.1.

Of 2 213 fish collected by seine and gillnet, 14 species were found. Lake Whitefish (68.2%), Longnose Sucker (6.8%), Goldeye (6.6%), Walleye (4.3%), Northern Pike (3.9%), Flathead Chub (2.8%), White Sucker (2.4%), Trout-Perch (2.2%) Arctic Grayling (1.1%), Mountain Whitefish (0.7%), Burbot (0.7%), Lake Chub (0.2%), Yellow Perch (0.1%), and Rainbow Trout (1 specimen). The Athabasca River between Fort McMurray and Cascade Rapids is a critical spawning habitat for Lake Whitefish. Lake Whitefish, and possibly Goldeye and Walleye, migrate between the study area and the Peace-Athabasca Delta, 300+ km away. Insects are consumed in large numbers by Goldeye, Lake and Mountain Whitefish, and Grayling. Pike and Walleye feed primarily on fish.

Machniak, K. and W.A. Bond. *An Intensive Study of the Fish Fauna of the Steepbank River Watershed of Northeastern Alberta.* Edmonton: Alberta Environment and Environment Canada, 1979.
Alberta Oil Sands Environmental Research Program Report 61, Project AF 4.5.2.

Fish that moved, from the Athabasca River, upstream for spring spawning included Longnose Suckers (52%), Arctic Grayling (20%) and White Suckers (14%). In the spring, Mountain Whitefish (7%) migrated upstream for feeding and movements of Northern Pike (3%) and Walleye (3%) were also recorded. Resident fish included Pearl Dace, Brook Stickleback, Lake Chub, Longnose Dace and Slimy Sculpin. Other fish recorded were: Lake Whitefish, Goldeye, Dolly Varden, Burbot, Trout-Perch, Flathead Chub, Lake Cisco, Redbelly Dace, Brassy Minnow, Spottail Shiner, Brook Stickleback, and Yellow Perch.

Machniak, K., W.A. Bond, M.R. Orr, D. Rudy and D. Millar. *Fisheries and Aquatic Habitat Investigations in the MacKay River Watershed of Northeastern Alberta.* Edmonton: Alberta Environment and Environment Canada, 1980. Alberta Oil Sands Environmental Research Program Report 93, WS 1.3.1.

Deals with fish migration and populations of the MacKay, Dover and Dunkirk Rivers. Similar findings as Machniak and Bond, 1979.

McCart, P., P. Tsui, W. Grant and R. Green. *Baseline Studies of Aquatic Environments in the Athabasca River near Lease 17. Volume 1: Baseline Studies.* Edmonton: Syncrude Canada Ltd., 1977?.
Environmental Research Monograph 1977-2.

Studies of the water quality, periphyton, benthic macroinvertebrates and fish.

McCart, P., P. Tsui, W. Grant, R. Green and D. Tripp. *Baseline Study of the Water Quality and Aquatic Resources of the MacKay River, Alberta.* Edmonton: Syncrude Canada Ltd., 1978?.
Environmental Research Monograph 1978-4.

Studies of the water quality, periphyton, benthic macroinvertebrates and fish.

Monenco Consultants Ltd. *Environmental Monitoring Studies in the Vicinity of the Peace River Pulp Mill Company Mill at Peace River, Alberta.* Calgary: Monenco Consultants Ltd., 1989, 1990.
Prepared for Daishowa Canada Co. Ltd.

Examples of macroinvertebrate and water quality surveys as required by the permit holder.

Monenco Consultants Ltd. *Winter Dissolved Oxygen Monitoring in the Vicinity of the Peace River Pulp Mill Company Mill at Peace River, Alberta. February, 1991.* Calgary: Monenco Consultants Ltd., 1991.
Prepared for Daishowa Canada Co. Ltd.

An example of a short term study of dissolved oxygen.

Noton, L.R. *The Peace and Athabasca River Systems: A Synopsis of Alberta Environment's Monitoring*

Noton, L.R. and R.D. Shaw. *Programs and the Water Quality Effects of Existing Pulp Mill Effluents.* Edmonton: Alberta Environment, Environmental Assessment Branch, Environmental Quality Monitoring Branch, 1989.

A 12 page overview.

Noton, L.R. and R.D. Shaw. *Winter Water Quality in the Athabasca River System, 1988 and 1989.* Edmonton: Alberta Environment, Environmental Protection Services, Environmental Assessment Branch, environment Quality Monitoring Branch, 1989.

A 200 page report.

Noton, L.R. and others. *Water Quality in the Wapiti-Smokey River System Downstream of the Procter and Gamble Pulp Mill, 1983.* Edmonton: Alberta Environment, Environmental Assessment Division, Environmental Quality Monitoring Branch, 1989.

Not seen.

Smith, Ann C. and William A. Yodis. *Environmental Auditing Quality Management.* New York: Executive Enterprises Publications, 1989.

A handbook for managing an environmental audit. Could be used to help prepare or critique a management plan.

Taylor, J.K. and T.W. Stanley, editors. *Quality Assurance for Environmental Measurements.* Philadelphia: ASTM Publications, 1985.

The results of a technical conference on monitoring air and water quality.

Thompson, M.S. and J. Crosby-Diewold. *Baseline Inventory of Aquatic Macrophyte Species Distributions in the AOSERP Study Area.* Edmonton: Alberta Environment and Environment Canada, 1980. Alberta Oil Sands Environmental Research Program Report 100, Project LS 10.2.

More than 10 lakes were surveyed to find the kinds (19+) and distributions of the large aquatic plants.

Tripp, D.B. and P.J. McCart. *Investigations of the Spring Spawning Fish Populations in the Athabasca and Clearwater Rivers Upstream from Fort McMurray. Volume 1.* Edmonton: Alberta Environment and Environment Canada, 1979. Alberta Oil Sands Environmental Research Program Report 84, Project WS 1.6.1

A basic study of the spawning of the major fish of these rivers.

Walder, G.L and D.W. Mayhood. *An Analysis of Benthic Invertebrate and Water Quality Monitoring Data from the Athabasca River.* Edmonton: Research Management Division, Alberta Environment, 1985.

A basic review.

Planning (see also EIA and Human Health)

Alberta Energy and Natural Resources, Resource Evaluation and Planning Division. *Resource Development Opportunities in Northern Alberta.* Edmonton: Alberta Energy and Natural Resources, 1985.
ENR Technical Report Number T/88.

An overview of statistics on socio-economics, transportation, forest resources, agriculture, petroleum and natural gas, oil sands, coal, fish and wildlife, water, and recreation for the northern half of the province.

Alberta Energy and Natural Resources, Resource Evaluation and Planning Division. *Big Bend Sub-Regional Integrated Resource Plan.* Edmonton: Alberta Energy and Natural Resources, 1985.

Agriculture, recreation, tourism, logging, hunting and mining plans for provincial lands located between Athabasca and Slave Lake.

Alberta, Government of. *A Policy for Resource Management of the Eastern Slopes.* Edmonton: Government of Alberta, revised 1984.
ENR number T/38, ISBN 0-86499-067-7.

Land use plans for the upper Athabasca River, around Hinton, are described.

Cairns, John Jr., editor. *Ecoaccidents.* New York: Plenum Press, 1985.

A NATO conference that reviews four case histories on ecological accidents, and outlines possible scenarios with oil spills and trichloroethylene.

Cashman, John R. *Hazardous Materials Emergencies: Response and Control.* Lancaster, PA.: Technomic, 1986.

Includes chapters on: public safety organizations, industrial response teams, commercial response organizations, training concerns, tools, and case histories of accidents.

DePol, Dennis R. *Emergency Response to Hazardous Materials Incidents.* Lancaster, PA.: Technomic, 1984.

Includes contingency planning, evacuation, emergency procedures, and emergency equipment. American rules and regulations.

Drabek, Thomas E. *Human System Responses to Disaster: An Inventory of Sociological Findings.* New York: Springer-Verlag, 1986.

Topics include: planning, warning, evacuation, emergency actions, restoration, reconstruction, perceptions of hazards, attitudes and adjustments, and disaster research. A good summary of research findings.

Greenprint for Canada Committee. *Greenprint for Canada: A Federal Agenda for the Environment.* Ottawa: Greenprint for Canada Committee (111 Sparks Street, 4th Floor, K1P 5B5), 1989.

An open appeal to the Prime Minister asking for reforms in policies, regulations, and institutions.

HAZTECH Canada Conference Planning Committee. *Dangerous Goods and Hazardous Waste Management Conference, Proceedings.* Mississauga, Ontario: Canadian Exhibition Management Inc. and Conference Planning Committee, 1988.

A mixture of papers on hazardous materials including: spills, emergency response, transportation, detection, risk assessment, and education. Be careful, some of them were trying to sell certain technologies.

Korten, David C. and Rudi Klauss, editors. *People-Centered Development: Contributions toward Theory and Planning Frameworks.* West Hartford, Connecticut: Kumarian Press, 1984.

Essays on development, some of which deal with environmental issues.

Whyte, Anne and Ian Burton. *Environmental Risk Assessment.* Toronto: John Wiley and Sons, 1980. Published on behalf of the Scientific Committee on Problems of the Environment (SCOPE) of the International Council of Scientific Unions (ICSU).

A primer on deciding between social benefits and environmental risk. Non-mathematical.

Pulp and Paper Mills (see also Air Pollution and Water Pollution)

Bamsey, C.R., editor. *Directory of Primary Wood-Using Industries in Alberta - 1988.* Edmonton: Forestry Canada and Alberta Forestry, Lands and Wildlife, 1988.

Names and addresses of the 306 firms (sawmills, planer mills, panelboard mills, wood treatment plants, and pulp and paper mills) that use cut logs in Alberta. Statistics for 1987 are provided for each firm as well as several useful appendices.

Eddie, Howard. *Environmental Control for Pulp and Paper Mills.* Park Ridge, N.J.: Noyes, 1984.

Good overview for air and water pollution but references are old.

Heimburger, Stanley A., Daniel S. Blevins, Joseph H. Bostwick and G. Paul Donnini. *Kraft Mill Bleach Plant Effluents: Recent Developments Aimed at Decreasing Their Environmental Impact. Parts 1 and 2.* Tappi Journal, volume 71, numbers 10 and 11?, pages 51-60 and 69-78, October and November 1986.

Covers extended and oxygen delignification, substitution of bleaching chemicals and process modifications.

Kirkpatrick, Neil. *Environmental Issues in the Pulp and Paper Industries: A Literature Review.* Leatherhead, Surrey, England: Pira Information Services, 1991.

Reviews environmental issues with respect to use of wood, pulping, bleaching, papermaking and recycling, biotechnology and legislation in the United Kingdom. There are 105 abstracts plus 18 additional references.

McCubbin, Neil. *The Basic Technology of the Pulp and Paper Industry and Its Environmental Protection Practices.* Ottawa: Environmental Protection Programs Directorate, Environment Canada, 1983.
Report EPS-6-EP-83-1.

This is a training manual written mainly from the environment protection point-of-view. It covers the importance and history of the industry in Canada, wood preparation, pulping, screening and cleaning, bleaching, stock preparation, paper machines and dryers, chemical recovery, steam and electrical generation, and effluent treatment. Its appendices include: chemical symbols, wood chemistry, and a glossary.

McCubbin, Neil. *State-of-the-Art of the Pulp and Paper Industry and its Environmental Practices.* Ottawa: Environment Canada, 1984.
Report EPS-3-EP-84-2.

A review of such topics as: forestry operations, debarking, pulping systems, chemical recovery, washing and screening, bleaching, papermaking, steam and power, effluents, computer applications, energy, and costs.

Miller Freeman Publishers. *Lockwood-Post's Directory of the Pulp, Paper and Allied Trades.* San Francisco, California: Miller Freeman, 1989.

Addresses of pulp and paper businesses in Canada and U.S.A.

Nghia, Hoc Tran. *Deposit Control Technology for Kraft Recovery Units.* Ottawa: Industrial Programs Branch, Environmental Protection Service, Environment Canada, 1984.
Report EPS 3/PF/1.

When the black liquor is burned in a recovery unit, the combustion products form deposits inside the unit. These deposits reduce the efficiency of the recovery unit. This paper describes an instrument that measures the amount of deposit accumulation.

Sandwell and Company. *Dead Load Reduction in the Kraft Pulping Process.* Industrial Programs Branch, Environmental Protection Service, Environment Canada, 1986.
Report EPS 3/PF/2.

Dead load refers to the amounts of non-reactive chemicals being re-cycled within the pulping process. This paper focuses on improving the efficiencies of the white liquor evaporation process at the Great Lakes Forest Products mill.

Science Council of Canada. *A Sectoral Approach to Innovation: The Case of the Forest-Product Industries.* Ottawa: Science Council of Canada, 1987.
Catalogue No. SS31-14/6-1987.

Recommendations to the Canadian industry to improve its technologies and increase research and development.

Thomas, Randy. *Pulp and Poison.* Monday Magazine, volume 15, number 3, cover, pages 6 - 9, 12-18 January 1989.

This article concentrates on the environmental problems of a pulp mill in Creston, British Columbia. It also covers the frustrations of ordinary people trying to deal with the pulp industry.

Woodbridge, Reed and Associates. *Aspen for High Quality Chemi-Mechanical Pulps: Overview for Alberta.* Vancouver: The company, 1981.

Use of poplar in an alternative process to Kraft bleaching.

Waste Management (see also Air Pollution and Water Pollution)

Beak Consultants Ltd. *Stripping Kraft Foul Condensates with Waste Gases.* Ottawa: Environment Canada, Environmental Protection Services, Water Pollution Control Directorate, 1982.

Not seen.

Brewer, Heather M. *Anaerobic Technology: A review of Research, Development and Demonstration Activity in the Agrifood and Pulp and Paper Industries.* Ottawa: Industrial Programs Branch, Environmental Protection, Conservation and Protection, Environment Canada, 1988.

Not seen.

Exner, Jurgen H., editor. *Solving Hazardous Waste Problems: Learning From Dioxins.* Washington, D.C.: American Chemical Society, 1987.

From a symposium held by the American Chemical Society in April 1986. Thirty-one papers on distribution, toxicology, risk assessment and risk management.

Freeman, Harry M., editor. *Innovative Thermal Processes for Treating Hazardous Wastes.* Lancaster, PA.: Technomic, 1986.

Covers such techniques as: wet oxidation, fluidized bed incineration, pyrolysis, electric reactors, plasma systems, chemical transformations and advanced incinerators.

Freeman, Harry M., editor. *Incinerating Hazardous Wastes.* Lancaster, PA.: Technomic, 1988.

A review of the thermal mechanisms for destruction of certain hazardous wastes.

Freeman, Harry M., editor. *Standard Handbook of Hazardous Waste Treatment and Disposal.* Montreal: McGraw-Hill, 1988.

Good overview of many topics, including: dioxins, various thermal processes, aerobic and anaerobic decomposition, landfill, and sampling.

Jank, B.E. et al. *An Assessment of Kraft Bleachery Effluent Toxicity Reduction Using Activated Sludge.* Ottawa: Water Pollution Control Directorate, 1977.

Not seen.

Malinen, Raimo, Nils-Erik Virkola and Esko Turunen. *Effluent Characterization and Treatment of Chemithermomechanical Pulping.* Helsinki, Finland: University of Helsinki, Laboratory of Pulping Technology, 1985.

Not seen.

Metcalf and Eddy Inc. *Wastewater Engineering: Treatment, Disposal, and Reuse,* 3rd ed. Revised by George Tchobanoglous and Franklin L. Brown. New York: McGraw-Hill, 1991.

Text on treatment techniques for municipal wastewater.

National Council of the Paper Industry for Air and Stream Improvement. *A Review of the Status of Development and Application of Groundwater Models for Prediction of Contaminated Transport of Materials Derived from Land Disposal of Solids and Liquids.* New York: The Council, March 1984.
Also available as Technical Bulletin 425.

Not seen.

National Council of the Paper Industry for Air and Stream Improvement. *Landfill Gas Generation, Migration, Monitoring and Control.* New York: the Council, May 1984.
Also as the Council's Technical Bulletin 431.

Not seen.

Reed, Sherwood C., E. Joe Middlebrooks, and Ronald W. Crites. *Natural Systems for Waste Management and Treatment.* Toronto: McGraw-Hill, 1988.

Mathematical factors for designing waste water treatment facilities, such as sludge ponds.

Reid, Ian C. *Policy for In-Plant Control of Adsorbable Organic Halides in Kraft Pulp Mill Effluent.* Edmonton: Alberta Environment, Standards and Approvals Division, 1989.

Operating policy.

Springer, Allan M. *Industrial Environmental Control: Pulp and Paper Industry.* New York: John Wiley and Sons, 1986.

General overview.

Water Pollution (see also Fish Toxicology and Waste Management)

A.A. Aquatic Research Limited. *Procedures and Methods for Evaluating Water Quality Changes in Receiving Streams: Technical Manual.* [Edmonton]: Alberta Environment, 1986.

Procedures for testing water samples.

Bonsor, Norman, Neil McCubbin and John B. Sprague. *Kraft Mill Effluents in Ontario.* Toronto: Ontario Ministry of the Environment, 1988.
Prepared for the Technical Advisory Committee, Pulp and Paper Sector of MISA (Municipal/Industrial Strategy for Abatement) and Ontario Ministry of the

Environment by the Expert Committee on Kraft Mill Toxicity.

The best overview on the kinds and sources of wastes produced by kraft types of pulp mills.

Cherwinsky, Christina and Don Murray. *Preliminary Investigation of Trace Contaminants in Pulp and Paper Mill Effluents.* Toronto: Queen's Printer for Ontario, 1986.
MICROLOG 87-01079, 2 fiche

Gives long lists of chemicals and groups of chemicals found in pulp mill effluents. Such chemicals cause, or are suspected of causing: toxicity to aquatic organisms, mutations, cancers, fish tainting, or taste and odour problems for drinking water.

Colodey, A.G. *Environmental Impact of Bleached Pulp and Paper Mill Effluents in Sweden, Finland, and Norway: Implications to the Canadian Environment.* Ottawa: Unpublished report IP-99 of Environment Canada, Conservation and Protection, Pacific and Yukon Region, 1989.

This report looks into what pollution impacts (especially on fish) may occur in Canada. There is a large annotated bibliography on the effects of pulp and paper mill effluents; also a short summary of human health effects of such mills.

Daishowa Canada Co. Ltd. *Peace River Kraft Pulp Mill: Water Quality and Fisheries Impact Analysis and Dioxin Evaluation.* Calgary: Monenco Consultants Limited, 1987.

This is a draft report.

Dioxin Committee (a Joint Committee of the Air Pollution Control Division and Solid Waste Processing Division). *Bibliography on Dioxins.* Alexandria, Virginia: American Society of Mechanical Engineers, 1987.

Not seen.

Eisler, Ronald. *Dioxin Hazards to Fish, Wildlife, and Invertebrates: A Synoptic Review.* United States Fish and Wildlife Service, U.S. Department of the Interior, 1986.
Biological Report 85 (1.8).
Contaminant Hazard Review number 8.

A concise introduction to the problems of dioxins in wildlife. Recommends a maximum of 0.01 ppt (parts per trillion) in water to protect aquatic life or 10-12 ppt in food items of wildlife.

Griffiths, W.H. and B.D. Walton. *The Effects of Sedimentation on the Aquatic Biota.* Edmonton: Alberta Environment and Environment Canada, 1978.
Alberta Oil Sands Environmental Research Program AF 4.9.1.

Reviews detrimental effects of increased suspended and settled sediments on fish, benthic invertebrates, and primary producers. Upper tolerance for fish is about 80-100 mg/L and as low as 10-15 mg/L for bottom invertebrates. Sediments can arise from vegetation removal, road construction, and industrial activities.

Haufe, W.O. *Control of Black Flies in the Athabasca River. Evaluation and Recommendations for Chemical Control of* Simulium arcticum *Malloch.* Edmonton: Alberta Environment, Pollution Control Division, 1980.

Addition of pesticides to the Athabasca River has many similarities to the addition of toxic effluents. This summary paper has a number of useful references.

Haufe, W.O. and G.C.R. Croome, editor. *Control of Black Flies in the Athabasca River. Technical report. An Interdisciplinary Study for the Chemical Control of* Simulium arcticum *Malloch in Relation to the Bionomics of Biting Flies in the Protection of Human, Animal, and Industrial Resources and its Impact on the Aquatic Environment.* Edmonton: Alberta Environment, Pollution Control Division, 1980.

Twenty-one papers related to application of methoxychlor to the Athabasca River. As stated above the behaviour of pesticides is similar to many toxic wastes.

Hogge, H.L. *Disposal of Waste Waters from Bleached Kraft Pulp Mills to the Athabasca River.* Edmonton: Alberta Department of Public Health, Division of Sanitary Engineering, April 1965.

A historical document.

Industrial Programs Branch, Environmental Protection Programs Directorate, Environmental Protection Service,

Environment Canada. *Status Report on Abatement on Water Pollution from the Canadian Pulp and Paper Industry (1982).* 1984. Ottawa: Environment Canada, 1984.
Report EPS 1/PF/1.

A short report on the industry's responses to federal government standards up to 1982. It includes: total suspended solids, biochemical oxygen demand, toxicity, sulphite pulping, compliance technology, research and development, effluents to municipal systems.

McLeay, D. and Associates Ltd. *Aquatic Toxicity of Pulp and Paper Mill Effluent: A Review.* Ottawa: Environment Canada, 1987.
Prepared for Environment Canada, Fisheries and Oceans Canada, Canadian Pulp and Paper Association, Ontario Ministry of the Environment.
Report EPS 4/PF/1.
MICROLOG 87-05110, 3 fiche

Excellent overview of chemicals, laboratory procedures, ecological effects, bioaccumulation, and bioassays.

Moore, James W. and S. Ramamoorthy. *Heavy Metals in Natural Waters.* New York: Springer-Verlag, 1984.

Production, transformations and toxicity of arsenic, cadmium, chromium, copper, lead, mercury, nickel and zinc.

Moore, James W. and S. Ramamoorthy. *Organic Chemicals in Natural Waters: Applied Monitoring and Impact Assessment.* New York: Springer-Verlag, 1984.

Includes production, behaviour and toxicity of: aliphatic hydrocarbons, aromatic hydrocarbons - monocyclics and polycyclics, chlorinated pesticides, petroleum hydrocarbons, phenols, polychlorinated biphenyls, and polychlorinated dibenzo-p-dioxins (PCDD).

National Council of the Paper Industry for Air and Stream Improvement. *Chlorinated Organics in Bleach Plant Effluents of Pulp and Paper mills.* New York: The Council, 1980.
Also available as the Council's Technical Bulletin 332.

Not seen.

Sachinath, Mitra. *Mercury in the Ecosystem.* Lancaster, PA.: Technomic, 1986.

Mercury seems to naturally occur in many lakes and rivers of Alberta. Some pulp mills used mercury to produce chlorine for bleaching. Though the mercury was supposed to be in a closed system, some escaped. Mercury compounds were formerly used in pulp mills as slimicides. This book explains how mercury moves around ecosystems.

Shaw, R.D. and l.R. Noton. *A Preliminary Assessment of the Impact of Existing Pulp Mills on the Peace River.* Edmonton: Alberta Environment, Environmental Protection Service, Environmental Assessment Division, Environmental Quality Monitoring Branch, 1989.

A 15 page summary.

Sprague, J.B. and A.G. Colodey. *Toxicity to Aquatic Organisms of Organochlorine Substances in Kraft Mill Effluents.* Ottawa: Unpublished report IP-100 of Renewable Resources, Extraction and Processing Division, Industrial Programs Branch, Conservation and Protection, Environment Canada, 1989.

This report gives information on lethal and sublethal effects of kraft effluents on various aquatic organisms as well as regulations for Europe and North America.

Trudel, L. *Dioxins and Furans in Bottom Sediments Near the 47 Canadian Pulp and Paper Mills Using Chlorine Bleaching.* Ottawa: Water Quality Branch, Inland Waters Directorate, Environment Canada, 1991.

These compounds were found at 95% of the sites. The high amounts found at some sites spurred the development of more stringent control regulations.

Van Strum, Carol and Paul Merrell. *No Margin of Safety: A Preliminary Report on Dioxin Pollution and the Need for Emergency Action in the Pulp and Paper Industry.* Greenpeace, 1987.

A review of the status of dioxins produced by the kraft pulping process.

Water: Rivers and Lakes (see also Monitoring)

Ash, G.R. and L.R. Noton. *A Fisheries and Water Quality Survey of Ten Lakes in the Richardson Tower Area, Northeastern Alberta. Volume I: Methodology, Summary, and Discussion.* Edmonton: Alberta Environment, 1980. Alberta Oil Sands Environmental Research Program Report 94, WS 1.4.1.

Basic descriptions of 10 lakes in the Richardson River and Grayling Creek basins. The lakes were not found to be highly susceptible to acidification.

Bramm, Susan, compiler. *A Bibliography of the Athabasca River Basin.* Edmonton: Alberta Environment Library, 1983.

125 pages.

Corley, N.T. et al., compilers. *A Selected Bibliography on the Peace and Athabasca Rivers and the Peace-Athabasca Delta Region.* Montreal: Arctic Institute of North America, 1971.

30 pages, dated.

Environment Canada. *Detailed Surface Water Quality Data. Alberta, Manitoba, Northwest Territories and Saskatchewan 1983.* Regina, Saskatchewan: Inland Waters Directorate. Western and Northern Region Water Quality Branch, 1985.

Gives results of tests (some done in the field and some in the laboratory) for various locations.

Hamilton, H.R., M.V. Thompson and L. Corkum. 1984. *Water Quality Overview of Athabasca River Basin.* Cochrane, Alberta: Nanuk Engineering and Development Ltd., 1985.
Prepared for Alberta Environment Planning Division.

Summarizes chemical data from Jasper, Athabasca and Fort McMurray (1970-1984) and six other surveys (1984-1985).

Limurg, Karin E., Mary Ann Moran and William H. McDowell. *The Hudson River Ecosystem.* New York: Springer-Verlag, 1986.

An ecological review of a river which is used by many industries and millions of people.

Moore, James W. *Balancing the Needs of Water Use.* London: Springer-Verlag, 1989. Springer Series on Environmental Management.

An introductory world view of water management.

Noton, L.R. and N.R. Chymko. *Water Quality and Aquatic Resources of the Beaver Creek Diversion System, 1977.* Edmonton: Syncrude Canada Ltd., 1978.
Environmental research Monograph 1978-3.

Plankton, invertebrate and fish studies of five aquatic habitats.

Peace-Athabasca Delta Implementation Committee, Canada, Alberta, Saskatchewan. *Peace-Athabasca Delta Water Management Works Evaluation. Final Report.* The committee, 1987.

The committee worked towards partially restoring water levels adversely affected by the W.A.C. Bennett Dam in British Columbia. Pollution of the Peace and Athabasca Rivers will affect this delta, which is a part of Wood Buffalo National Park.

Peace-Athabasca Delta Implementation Committee, Canada, Alberta, Saskatchewan. *Peace-Athabasca Delta Water Management Works Evaluation. Appendix B, Biological Assessment.* The committee, 1987.

Presents data on vegetation, fish, birds and mammals.

Peace-Athabasca Delta Project Group, Canada, Alberta, Saskatchewan. *The Peace-Athabasca Project.* Edmonton: The committee, 1973.
Technical Report: A report on low water levels in Lake Athabasca and their effects on the Peace-Athabasca Delta.
Technical Appendices. Volume 1: Hydrologic Investigations.
Technical Appendices. Volume 2: Ecological Investigations.
Technical Appendices. Volume 3: Supporting Studies. (Historical, Socio-economic, and Recreation-Tourism studies.)

The initial studies on the delta after the Bennett Dam was built.

Scarpino, Philip V. *Great River: An Environmental History of the Upper Mississippi, 1890-1950.* Columibia: Univ. of Missouri, 1985.

> Perhaps someone will to do a similar study of the Peace or Athabasca Rivers?

Smith, S.B. *The Peace-Athabasca Delta: a Choice of Water Management Alternatives.* Edmonton: Alberta Environment, 1973.

> An old paper but it has some information on the people and resources at the mouth of the Athabasca River.

Speidel, D.H., L.C. Ruedisili and A.F. Agnew, editors. *Perspectives on Water: Uses and Abuses.* New York: Oxford University Press, 1988.

> An introduction to water: its properties, role in the ecosphere, human uses and abuses, as well as legal, economic and management issues in the U.S.A.

Task Force on Water Quality Guidelines of the Canadian Council of Resource and Environment Ministers. *Canadian Water Quality Guidelines.* Ottawa: The committee, 1987.

> Standards on water quality.

Tripp, D.B. and P.T.P. Tsui. *Fisheries and Habitat Investigations of Tributary Streams in the Southern Portion of the AOSERP Study Area. Volume I.* Edmonton: Alberta Environment and Environment Canada, 1980.
Alberta Oil Sands Environmental Research Program Report 92, WS 1.6.2.

> Baseline studies of Algar, Horse, Hangingstone, Gregoire and Christina Rivers.

Wallis, P., E. Peake, M. Strosher, B. Baker and S. Telang. *The Assimilative Capacity of the Athabasca River for Organic Compounds.* Edmonton: Alberta Oil Sands Environmental Research Program Project WS 2.3.2, 1980.

> One of the findings of this report is that the most productive time of the year for the lower Athabasca River is the winter, when flow and turbidity are low and numbers of phytoplankton and animals are high.

Yau, H., K.L. Murphy and P.L. Timpany. *Athabasca River Modelling Studies (Phase 1): Fort McMurray - Embarras.* Edmonton: Alberta Oil Sands Environmental Research Program and Alberta Environment, 1982.
Prepared by International Environmental Consultants Ltd. for Research Management Division.
Alberta Oil Sands Environmental Research Project Report L-76.

> Use of a mass balance approach to model movement of dissolved chlorine, total alkalinity and total hardness in the lower Athabasca River.